S P R I N G   S N O W

FROM *The Old Farmer's Almanac*

Illustrations by Abigail Rorer

Spring Snow

THE SEASONS OF
NEW ENGLAND

CASTLE FREEMAN, JR.

A PETER DAVISON BOOK

Houghton Mifflin Company

BOSTON   NEW YORK

1995

For information about permission to reproduce selections from this book, write to Permissions, Houghton Mifflin Company, 215 Park Avenue South, New York, New York 10003.

For information about this and other Houghton Mifflin trade and reference books and multimedia products, visit The Bookstore at Houghton Mifflin on the World Wide Web at http://www.hmco.com/trade/.

Library of Congress Cataloging-in-Publication Data

Freeman, Castle (Castle W.)
Spring snow : the seasons of New England
from the Old farmer's almanac / Castle Freeman, Jr. :
illustrations by Abigail Rorer.
p. cm.
"A Peter Davison book."
Includes index.
ISBN 0-395-73098-8
1. Natural history — New England. 2. Country life — New
England. 3. Season — New England. I. Title.
QH104.5N4F74   1995
508.74—dc20   95-17170   CIP

Printed in the United States of America

QUM 10 9 8 7 6 5 4 3 2 1

Book design by Anne Chalmers
Text type is New Baskerville (Adobe)
Display type is Bulmer (Monotype)

All the essays in this book were originally published as the monthly "Farmer's
Calendar" in The Old Farmer's Almanac, copyright © 1981, 1982, 1983,
1984, 1985, 1986, 1987, 1988, 1989, 1990, 1991, 1992, 1993,
1994, 1995, Yankee Publishing Incorporated.

Preface & Advertisement

EVEN TODAY— especially today — it is a first principle of New England, and so also of its historic encyclopedia, *The Old Farmer's Almanac*, to give value for money. In *Spring Snow* we have done that. The volume you hold is not only a book; it's also a zoo, a garden, an aviary, a museum, a junkyard, a library, a college, a nursery, and an observatory.

In the pages that follow, then, are twenty-six wild mammals, twenty-two birds, three reptiles, two amphibians, and seventeen insects. There are sixteen kinds of tree, six wildflowers, four tame flowers, fourteen kinds of garden vegetable, one comet, one star of the first magnitude, and two constellations.

All are found in a setting that is remarkable for its uniformity and for its rigor: the "Farmer's Calendar" column in *The Old Farmer's Almanac*. For the writers whose job it has been to fill that column in the two hundred years of the *Almanac*'s existence, the space presents a challenge akin to that of building a scale model of the *Mayflower* inside a miniature bottle of airline Scotch. You have a hole of about nine square inches, the size of an old-fashioned mail slot, a matter of 325 words. You're to fill it — twelve times. What do you do?

In the part of its long life — much the greater part — when *The Old Farmer's Almanac* was read largely by real farmers, that

question had an easy answer. You set up the old stand first oper-
ated two thousand years ago by Virgil and various Ancient
Greeks: practical agricultural advice. I have before me the *Old
Farmer's Almanac* for 1874. In the "Farmer's Calendar" for June,
the author writes:

> I hope you have a good piece for Swedish turnips.
> Now is the time to put in the seed, say the twentieth
> or twenty-fifth of this month. The Swedes make a
> good crop for feeding out in the early part of the
> winter.

Good, sound advice, coming as it plainly does from a store of ac-
tual experience and care — but of limited use, perhaps, to most
readers of *The Old Farmer's Almanac* as it enters its third century.
We farm otherwise today. We don't plant Swedes. We may wonder whether the Swedes, or some of their neighbors, will not one
day be planting us.

It seemed best to the *Almanac*'s editors, therefore, to allow the
"Farmer's Calendar" to forget a little its utilitarian ancestry and
put in the place of real knowledge impression, reflection, some
book learning, and a good deal of fancy. Clearly they needed,
not a farmer any longer, but a Constant Reader with a sideline in
what used to be called Natural History, an impractical, unsystem-
atic, unemployed beneficiary and victim of the liberal arts education as it was known thirty years ago. They hired me in 1981, and
we have gone on happily together ever since.

There are in *Spring Snow* four great books, two scary movies,
three heroes of fiction, one business executive, one general, and
two European aristocrats. One of these noblemen, however, I
made up. I also made up, I'm afraid, both of the Far Eastern
philosophers who appear here; but there are seven poets and
their lines, and every one of them is real. There are eleven great
scientists, also real, and ten great authors.

One of the last, unsurprisingly, is Henry David Thoreau
(1817–1862), of Concord, Massachusetts, who visits these pages
briefly twice. I confess I have always thought Thoreau must have
been in life a vain, difficult, indeed insufferable man, but he is
the author of *Walden; or Life in the Woods* (1854), one of the three

or four unmistakably great works of American letters. There he writes that he has "traveled a good deal in Concord." It's a pointed remark. Thoreau lived among people for whom foreign travel — lately having become relatively safe and easy — was an important part of education. He spurned it, famously sticking close to his little hometown some miles west of Boston. As far as I can learn, Thoreau didn't venture beyond a hundred miles from that spot more than half a dozen times from the beginning of his life to its end.

In its devotion to its own, single place, and in its confidence in the riches of that place, *Spring Snow* is in the same tradition. There are here, finally, one old house painted red (not recently enough), twenty-two acres of foothill land, three meadows, two woodlots, one brook, one vegetable patch, three flower beds, six cats, one dog, two children, two grownups, four or five neighbors, and the life of something like seven thousand days.

Our book is a multitude, then, but it hasn't much of the exotic, not much of the adventurous or the strange; instead, small, familiar matters and everyday occasions available to anybody — available to anybody, that is, who will hold still. I have read someplace that most Americans move every five years. This book is not for them. Or, yes it is: it's for them especially. It's for them more and more.

Spring Snow is a book about staying put.

Not in these pages, exactly, but behind them, are also six men and women. Every author who is lucky enough to secure a publisher for his work finds himself in an enterprise that is necessarily a collaboration, something authors discover with degrees of horror, insult, resignation, relief, and gratitude. For me, gratitude rules, in particular as follows: Susan Peery, Jud Hale, Tim Clark, and Debra Sanderson of *The Old Farmer's Almanac* have been generous in their support and encouragement of my writing the "Farmer's Calendar" over fourteen years and more. Christina Ward, my friend and literary agent, carried the idea of a collection of these columns successfully through the thickets of the publishing industry, where their author had not the wit or nerve to cut a path. Peter Davison of Houghton Mifflin Company has been the most thorough and astute reader these columns have had. Much of what is happiest and most distinctive in their organization and selection in this book is owing to him. Also at Houghton Mifflin, Jayne Yaffe has edited the manuscript of this collection with a care that has improved the text in ways nobody knows better, or appreciates more, than I. Abigail Rorer has contributed engravings whose accuracy, attentiveness, and charm I hope the columns at their best are equal to. Carol Barber of West Brattleboro, Vermont, helped me with finding plants when my knowledge of the local woodlands failed. Alice Freeman has furnished either in life or by suggestion the subjects of several of these columns. She has read them all, mostly as they were written. She has praised the ones she liked, and about the others she has held her peace. No author, no mate, can hope for better treatment than that, and most have to settle for less. My thanks to all.

CASTLE FREEMAN, JR.
Newfane, Vermont
March 1995

Spring

The Look of the Land

H O W do the meadows green? By the end of April the lank brown fields, flattened and bleached by the winter snow, have been overtaken by strong spring green. If you watch over a particular meadow during this month, you will find the increase of green is a process you can notice, but one you can't measure or observe. In the same way, you can't observe the aging of familiar faces, including your own, though you can see it plainly at certain times. In April, youth and renewal surprise a meadow by a kind of reversal of the same elusive process as that by which our age surprises us. It's another instance in which, to a certain eye, nature goes up and down, forward and back, by the same steps.

The meadows green by a slow suffusion. Lowland meadows turn to green before upland; and everywhere short grass greens earliest. By mid-April clipped lawns and borders show a deep summer green, while mowings and open fields are still in late winter's pale straw. In them the green comes up from under. Some meadows green irregularly, in patches and points. For a day or so an April meadow may take on the look of a map with continents, peninsulas, and islands of green in oceans of brown. Some meadows green late. I drive by one big hillside that shows its open, curved top to the southwest and never seems to wake at all much before May Day. Each meadow has its own plan, its own clock.

As a meadow quickens, there will be an hour when the quantity of new green just balances winter's brown and grays. Then the spring's green will seem to light the old meadow from below, making it momentarily luminous. This phenomenon lasts for a day or less. A gentle rain will come to aid the new grass, and the next day the meadow will be entirely green.

LAST month the sun, mounting the southern sky, crossed the vernal equinox, and now it has a clear shot at the earth. Along the roads the snow goes down quickly; in the woods it melts away. Foot trails that people made across the snow now reappear for a day, then turn to mud. Brooks, rivers, ponds open; their banks soften; the ice that held them floats on the water, turns, bobs, is carried away.

Now, before the trees begin to leaf, before the grass begins to turn green and grow, the land is unguarded. Get out and see it. Find a hillside, sit down, and look over the country.

The air is cold, but already the wind smells of plant life, growth, and earthworms. The land looks like a patchwork cover worked years ago by a stern old wife who distrusted bright colors and fancy patterns. She patched simple rectangles, mostly, of common cloth and in common colors. Hardwood stands are brown; above them the belts of softwoods are soft green. Cornfields are a kind of dun color from the brown mud and the gray or brown of last year's stubble. Meadows are tan, the color of a pale fox. Where people have their gardens the patches are a fine, rich black. Only where gardeners and farmers planted cover crops last year is there now bright color, intensely green.

When the snow goes away for the last time, it goes first from under pines and hemlocks that grow on hillsides turned toward the south. There the ground is warm and dry. You can sit and admire the season. It's one of the shortest of them all. In a week the world will be green. Even today, although the nights are cold, if you're outdoors at evening you'll hear in the woods a single peeper sounding the same note slowly, regularly, over and over again like a bored kid dinging away at a piano.

April 10. Went down to the train depot at Springfield and boarded the Yankee Clipper to Washington, D.C., a seven-hour shot. It's an interesting ride that seems to pack a great deal of geography into a small compass. You go right down the Connecticut River to New Haven. Then you make a right and go along the top of Long Island Sound toward New York. Somewhere in what must be the Borough of Queens, you descend and pass under Manhattan, emerging in New Jersey. There you turn left and proceed to Philadelphia, across the river mouths emptying into Chesapeake Bay, and so into Washington, a southern city.

The best part of the trip for me is the Long Island Sound leg, say from Bridgeport to near New York. Here the train passes through the backyard of the old industrial America. It's not pretty. There would seem to be nobody home here these days. You pass every kind of factory, plant, shop, dock, most of them apparently vacant, their windows broken, their signs faded, their fences fallen down. You're riding through an industrial ruin seventy-five miles long, a district uniformly, relentlessly ugly.

Yet I'm reminded of the lines of the poet: "And for all this, nature is never spent; / There lives the dearest freshness deep down things; . . ." A beautiful, cold, early spring day with high clouds, a keen wind, bright sun. The grimy trackside tree-of-heaven and tangled brush behind the conked-out plants are coming in green. And, most remarkable, most unexpected: swans. So help me, all along the rail line in every stagnant backwater and pool, however filthy, floating placidly among the old tires, busted concrete, and other junk, a perfect, snow-white swan. Where do they come from?

Tools & Tasks

I DROVE my trash to the town dump the other day and narrowly missed being creamed by one of the town fathers, whose pickup, barely under control, was careening past the old-newspapers drop. As he barreled past my side I thought I heard the old gentleman let out a whoop. Then, at the dump's landfill, where you leave the trash, I had to pull well back to stay out of the way of an elderly lady who was trying to burn rubber in the mud as she pulled away from the fill, her wheels spinning, and zoomed toward the gate.

Something in the air of a town dump causes ordinarily law-abiding and even sedate citizens to lose their inhibitions. They zing about the muddy tracks and among the hills of refuse with an abandon worthy of a demolition derby. Perhaps it's some exhalation from the tire pile or the smoke from burning mattresses that leads the precincts of a dump each Saturday morning to take on the rush and danger of a tatterdemalion motocross. Perhaps it's a more subtle influence: the high spirits everybody gets from sloughing off, if only for an hour, some of the material trappings — the trash — that weigh him down. Like strong young horses that have just been let out of their traces and given the run of the pasture, people who have dumped their week's stuff need to race around a bit and kick up their heels — and why not?

Whatever produces the dump-derby effect, it can really get the folks around here revved up. Having driven cautiously through the gate, they put the accelerator to the floor and let it wail. Where else can you surprise a selectman in full skid around the scrap metal or meet a member of the board of civil authority shooting in a storm of mud past the dead refrigerators?

SEVERAL years ago when the snow went out, I found that a portion of one of the old stone walls near our house had fallen badly. The wall in that section wasn't more than waist high, and only a few of the stones were big, so I decided that repairing the fallen part was a job I could take on. Not that I expected the work to be easy, mind you, or the end result as good as new. Making the round, knobby granite cobbles of my hill form up and hold their places in a good wall takes more art than I will ever have, I know well. Still, I thought, I didn't have to build a wall here, only rebuild one. The hard work had already been done: the stones had been laid up so as to stay put — until now. It only remained for me to put them back more or less where they'd been.

I set to it. A Vermont field rock the size of a footstool is the stubbornest, heaviest object in the universe. The idea that millions of these things are floating around in space as potential meteorites, light as thistledown, is absolutely untenable. I shoved the stones into place, wrestled them about so they lay quiet, wedged them in place with smaller stones. Presently the wall was back up.

But I was puzzled. I had six or seven stones left over. The wall looked not great, but pretty thrifty, I thought. Why, then, were there still unused stones? I was reminded of when I was little and used to take cheap pocket watches apart. I'd reassemble the scores of pieces, but always there would be a wheel, a pin, a spring too many. As many times as I'd dismantle a watch and put it together again, I'd have excess parts. My new wall was the same: it was whole, but it wasn't complete. Of course, I reflected, my new wall worked; my new watches, never.

First Insects

I WAS out for a walk one March day some years ago when I found a place where it looked as if someone had thrown a handful of iron filings or ground black pepper down on the snow. I took a closer look and found a patch of minute black grains scattered thickly over the snow. I knelt down close to get a good look. There was just time to note that each grain of the black dust was a little smaller than the small letter "o" on this page when something happened. The grain of dust I was looking at vanished. It was there and then it wasn't there. I found another grain. Shortly it too vanished. I stood up and soon saw that the handful of black pepper on the snow was really some enormous number of *beings* that were continually hopping or flipping about. *This is something,* I thought.

It is at this point in experience that you go to books, there to find that the marvel you've happened on is a commonplace. My disappearing pepper is an insect called the snow flea *(Achorutes nivicolus)*, a northern member of the big group of insects called springtails. These little guys are shaped like tiny grains of rice, and at their back end they have a stiff tail that bends around underneath them and is held in tension by a catch on their belly. Imagine an upside-down mousetrap, set. Released, the tail snaps the snow flea up and back, and they are so small that the sudden movement makes them appear to vanish. They develop from an immature form, a nymph, in the late winter and creep up through the snow to throng on the surface in the earliest spring sun, animated dust that puzzles the sap gatherers in the maple bush, if they aren't too busy to notice. Like any other bug, snow fleas love what's sweet. You can find them swimming around in the sap buckets.

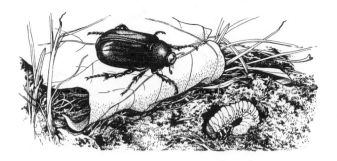

Turn up a spadeful of earth in your garden, and there is one of those fat, brown-headed grubs the size and shape of a tightly curled little finger and colored like old ivory. Like a snake, it looks slimy but is really dry and perfectly clean. It was from garden grubs like these that I first learned not everybody liked to handle things that came up out of the dirt as much as I did.

Garden grubs are a sign of spring in that it's spring when we spade our gardens and discover them; but in fact the earth is full of grubs in all seasons. The fat-little-finger grubs that I know best are the larvae of June bugs, the noisy brown beetles that barnstorm around lighted windows on spring nights. Their fancy name is *Phyllophaga*. The bug books say there are more than a hundred species of June bugs. They lay eggs in little hollows they make underground in gardens, fields, and lawns. The grubs hatch from the eggs and live underground for two or three years eating plant roots. I can't imagine the grubs get around much underground, for they don't seem to be built for travel. If you look, though, you'll see that they do have little grasping arms in front like a caterpillar's; caterpillars are really what these grubs are. In their third fall they become pupae for the winter, and next spring the pupae produce new June bugs.

In my childhood we used to prize garden grubs for fishing. When you spitted one on your hook, it never seemed to mind, a fact that always made me doubt their value as bait. How can so dull a creature entice? Still, it was well known that grubs were death on bass, far superior to other lures. I myself have never caught a bass with a garden grub, however. I try and try. But then, in the pond where I go bass fishing there are no bass.

MAY is the big yellow butterflies' time. They are tiger swallowtails *(Papilio glaucus),* black-barred yellow and as big as a boy's hand. The tigers are about the largest butterflies that northern New England has. They turn up around the middle of the month in my neighborhood, and for some weeks they are everywhere. They are about the meadows and gardens, but they also love the woods, and it seems that every step you take there will start up another one to fly before you among the rays of sunlight that get in between the trees. The butterflies frequent the roadsides, too, and there thousands of them come to grief, done in by cars. You can find their bright wings decorating your radiator when you return from a drive.

In a good swallowtail year you can hardly look out at the world from any quarter without seeing one of these butterflies passing in lazy flight. By July enough of them will have been snapped up by birds, killed by misfortunes of one kind or another, and inhaled by automobiles so that they won't appear as common. Now, however, these big butterflies dominate the lengthening May days like yellow-winged summer thoughts.

The tiger swallowtail comes from a caterpillar, a green thing about an inch long with a humped back and a pair of yellow pop eyes that aren't really eyes (they'd be on its shoulders if caterpillars had shoulders). Even among caterpillars this one is nothing special; it's unassuming and unlovely, and it doesn't do any of those little tricks that distinguish some other caterpillars. And yet from this unpromising material will come a creature splendid, famed, and powerful in its way. It's that contrast that prompts the last of the sage's Seven Questions. Asked of the caterpillar, that question is: *Does it know?*

Change

MARCH is like a school play. The fond audience is gathered and expectant; they are eager for the performance to commence. On stage there are sounds of fevered activity, but everything is hidden behind the curtain, which has not yet gone up. The audience must wait a little longer, but they can while away the time by trying to recognize and interpret the bumps, scrapings, and muffled shrieks that issue from behind the curtain, and by watching for a kid to peep out at them.

In March the play we await is the spring, and the signs of its approach, though many, are small and are almost overwhelmed by the remaining evidences of winter. It's as though the scenery and props for spring are being secretly prepared, and all the actors are taking their places under the snow so that when winter finally goes, the new season will be set up and ready to begin. You have to look and listen for spring's March preparations, but the signs are there if you do. Some butterflies hibernate, and a warm March sun will bring them out. You'll see them flying sleepily over the snow. Raccoons are out, too. Having slept away the worst of winter, they are abroad these nights. The woods are deep in snow still, but the buds of the beeches are sharp and shiny; the buds of the shagbarks are like great wax flowers. If you listen in the woods, you can hear faint calls and whispers: the brooks are running again beneath the ice.

On the hillsides and on banks beside the roads where the sun hits, there are dark patches on the snow. That's dirt, earth. You don't recognize it at first because it's been four or five months since you have seen bare ground in any quantity. There it is, though, one of the young company of spring peeping out at you from the other side of the curtain like that kid at the play.

ALL around the bend in the river road, cars are pulled over to the side, and on the bridge eight or ten people have gathered. They come and go all day. They're gawking at the ice. The breaking up of the frozen waters and the departure of the ice down the rivers is winter's last big show, and often it makes a mighty spectacle, a view of the underside of winter, the engine room, the groaning, grinding machinery.

The river down the road from where I live is no more than 150 feet across at the point where it makes a bend following which the channel widens out some. There the ice, floating down from upriver, is apt to get stuck. A dam of ice begins to rise. More and more ice comes down the river, meets the dam, tries to push through it, fails, tries to climb over it, fails. The dam grows deeper, higher. It looks like a Corps of Engineers project built up of riprap blocks. These engineers are not men, though, but giants. The ice blocks are prodigious. The little ones are the size of billiard tables, king-size beds. The big ones are half tennis courts. They are four, five feet thick, gray in color or green, sometimes a kind of pale blue like the spring sky.

The weight of the ice sheets is unimaginable, and yet the force that moves them along seems to toss them like cards. They are flung up crazily, at all angles, on the dam. They are shot out to the sides of the channel, where they scour the riverbanks and mow down good-sized trees. As big as the ice blocks are, what is pushing them is bigger. They will go where they are pointed, and there is not too much that can stop them. The people watch silently, respectfully, from a safe distance.

MORE than any of the other eleven, March is the test month. It is the most sensitive indicator among the months of what the characteristic local climate and weather are. It is like a quivering, poised needle, which a few miles of latitude or a few hundred feet of elevation can tip back into winter or release into indubitable spring.

I live in the southern quarter of Vermont. Here the snow is on the ground through March. The deepest cold has passed, and the trees show spring buds, but there are always one or two snowstorms still to come. If you're a gardener around here, you can start seeds inside this month, but don't even think about planting them outside. In Illinois, however, where I have also lived, the crocuses are out, and the kids take their coats off coming home from school, although it's not exactly warm. The snow is gone. In Pennsylvania you can get warm in March, you can plant your garden, and some of the flowering trees are coming out. You can move your inside plants onto the porch and leave them there for eight or nine months. I have never been to the South in March. I imagine people down there sitting on the veranda, drinking juleps and swatting flies and wondering why the Vermonters haven't gone home.

These are big March effects, visible as you travel up and down a continent. More satisfactory are the little effects that you can see in your own backyard. Where the land lies along the wider rivers in my neighborhood, there is snow now, but it's old and sunken snow, and in patches it has given way to mud. March is essentially a spring month in the lowlands, even in the north. Twenty miles away along a road in the mountains things are different: the snowbanks are still above your head. The hardwoods haven't dared to bud. March is a winter month up there.

EVERY spring there is one last all-out snowstorm, but this time people don't meet the weather with any of the varieties of resignation they have perfected over a long winter of successive snows. This time a big snowfall is, well, funny. Spring blizzards are a lark. Why? Snow is snow: if you're sick of it in February, you ought by rights to be even sicker of it in April. Besides, spring blizzards — at least around here — are often among the biggest storms of the year in terms of inches dumped. Last year we had two feet in one April storm. Oughtn't their volume alone to make them particularly oppressive, never mind their timing?

No. This argument starts from a false premise, that snow is all alike. It isn't. Every snow is different, and the big spring snow is the most different of all. That heavy accumulation doesn't weigh on your soul; on the contrary, the magnitude of a spring blizzard is one of the aspects of it that make it a joke. These storms are like an outrageous dessert that winds up a seven-course dinner: General Grant life-size in blue ice cream at the G.A.R. banquet.

And anyway, you can enjoy anything if you know it isn't real. Spring blizzards are like painted scenes of storefronts on a stage set. You enter the illusion knowing you could punch your fist right through the brick walls, knowing that very soon someone will come and pack all the sets away. These are white storms. The sky is bright in spite of the snow, and the sun that will be out tomorrow is a spring sun that means business: in a day all this snow will be gone. You needn't take it seriously, then. The birds don't. The summer birds have already arrived, and you can hear the robins singing through the middle of the storm.

RISING above the shrinking snow, the horns of a bull, the prow of a ship, a spear, an urn. As the winter's full depth of snow sinks down farther and farther through the spring days, forgotten objects appear, like the roofs and towers of Atlantis emerging from the waves.

In this neighborhood the snow can cover the ground for four or five months. When it melts, it gives you the world back again, changed in some ways and in other ways embarrassingly the same. What evidence of careless householding the departing snow reveals at my place each spring! What tools, crockery, articles of clothing, toys, summer furniture show up — all of them, necessarily, un-put-away last year. And how do they *get to* where they seem for several months to have been?

Of course you expect to find the rake and a length of old string in the garden when the snow leaves it. I may even have put the string there on purpose last fall — at least I'll say I did. But I have found a sock in the meadow, a hat at the edge of the lawn, a garden chair up in the pines, a cup and saucer under the butternut tree, a doll above the driveway, plant pots virtually everywhere, and a copy of *Great Expectations* under the stone wall.

I think of the miscellany of baggage that turns up after the snow has gone as corresponding to the citizens of New England who spend the winter in Florida. Both stick around to enjoy the autumn — our finest season — and are last seen when the weather begins to turn nasty. Neither has ever sent me a postcard. Both the paraphernalia and the people reappear in the spring looking more or less the same, maybe a little older. Not that the correspondence is exact: the stuff I forgot last fall doesn't come back with a tan, and my copy of *Great Expectations* was a total loss, unfortunately.

T H E year turns to full spring, and some days look exactly like summer, but in protected places the last of the winter's snow can still be found. Under north walls, in cold hemlock thickets, beside fallen trunks in the woods, the old snow lies in scattered atolls that dwindle away like the last remnants of the submerged continent of winter. The old snow is icy, gray, coarse. It is stained and dirty, full of fallen pine needles and bits of bud scales and other trash.

Coming on a patch of old snow in the green woods in May is a surprise, and it's an embarrassment: as though you met a beggar in the street whom you knew to be the last unfortunate representative of a once aristocratic family now fallen into decay. Four months ago snow was everywhere. It ruled and its reign was splendid, the whole world its ermine robe; but now it's overthrown and it has fled into exile in the cool shadows, where it wastes away. You can imagine the old snow remembering its lost glory. Listen for it mumbling away like a senile Cavalier dreaming of Bonnie Prince Charlie and the Forty-Five.

Old snow hides in the same places every year. Around my house I know there will be a lump of it beside the north wall of our shed when dandelions have begun to grow in the grass a few feet away, and I know a place in the angle of a stone wall in the woods where the snow may remain into June. Some curious place names in this area have come from the old settlers' noticing that the snow and ice endured long past their natural term in dark, deep defiles where the sun never lingered. So we have Greenland Gulf, the Freezing Hole, and Frigid Ridge — although I confess that the old settler who named the last of these was I.

Flowers & Others

IN the first days of May, along with the daffodil, appears the red trillium *(Trillium erectum)*. It grows out of the old stone walls and out of the moist black soil of the cool woods. It's a vigorous plant a foot or more high with three broad leaves atop its stalk and in their axis the slightly drooping flower. The red-brown flower is a plain thing. It's distinguished not by its look but by its scent, which is uniquely terrible, a kind of strong, rank smell as of dead mice.

Its powerful reek sets this flower apart and, oddly enough, seems to win it friends. There's an old saying to the effect that a well-loved child has many names, and if it's true then this trillium must be a favorite. Books on wild plants give at least sixteen different common or local names for *T. erectum.* Two of the more memorable names — stinking Benjamin and wet-dog trillium — come from the flower's outrageous smell. Others allude to the plant's supposed medicinal properties. It is thought to aid in childbirth, and the Indians used it for snakebite — hence birthroot, Indian balm, squawroot.

Another name for this flower is *wake-robin,* a name that seems to me to be an example of the highest folk poetry. What does it mean? It sounds as though it meant that the trillium's blooming coincides with, and thus somehow signals, the spring arrival of the robin. But it doesn't, at least not around here; when our wake-robin comes out, the robins have been here for weeks. I think the robin who is fancifully being waked by *T. erectum* is not a bird but a boy, a man — Robin, in particular, a simple country fellow, a plowman, whose busy season on the land this flower's bloom announces.

UNDER the meager shade of the budding trees the blood-root pokes up through the cover of dead leaves at the base of the stone wall, in the woods opening, along the roadside. It is never a common flower, although it sometimes spreads to cover areas of several square yards or more.

The leaf is strange: single, round, deeply lobed, it looks delicate though strong, like kid leather. When the bloodroot first emerges in the early spring, the leaf is curled close about the single flower, and the plant looks like a hand sheltering a candle from the wind. The flower is white with slender petals on a weak stem. It closes up its petals at night, and the leaf also folds to encase the flower, which lasts about four days before the petals fall. After the flower fails, the leaves multiply and expand.

The bloodroot's flower and habit of growth make it resemble a hepatica, anemone, or other member of the buttercup family, but in fact it's a poppy. Its Latin name is *Sanguinaria canadensis,* and it is also called *puccoon,* from an Algonquin word related to words for blood and dye. All the names refer to the plant's juice, which is red or orange and which flows freely when the plant is injured, especially from the root.

European settlers were quick to notice the bloodroot. It was described from Virginia as early as 1640. Perhaps the colonists were especially aware of the plant because of its importance to the Indians. Indians of the eastern forests used the juice of the bloodroot as a dye and body paint, and they believed it had medicinal value against snakebite. It was practically inevitable that they should have given great importance to a plant with the curious, fleshy leaves of the bloodroot, especially one that issued blood like a man's.

Roads

"HOW's your mud?" people ask me. "How is it up there, pretty deep?" In the past I would have bragged. I would have said something like "Don't know if it's deep; haven't found the bottom yet." Nowadays I make some noncommittal answer: "Not too bad," I say, or, "Yes, it's a little soft today." I have learned that my friends don't admire my mud. Many of them regard mud–encumbered Marches and Aprils with something near scorn.

The issue, after all, is not mud as mud, not mud *per se*. Mud is everywhere, and nobody cares. When you think about it, the Earth itself is mostly mud, more or less dried up. Nobody objects. No, the issue is not mud; the issue is roads. Over much of the country, or as much of it as is subject to freezing and thawing, the civilizers have been at work for long enough so that today roads axle deep in spring mud are a part of remote history, like runaway teams. Even quiet country roads are usually paved — not well paved, always, not recently paved, but still relatively black, relatively hard.

Not in my state. Here we like dirt roads. I have never been entirely sure why, but I hope the reason is a principled reluctance to squander the taxpayer's dollar on fripperies (and an inability as yet to figure out how to get the Feds to pick up the paving tab). Whatever the reason, my little town, typical of Vermont, contains about seventy miles of roads, of which some three-quarters are dirt. Roads that in any other state would glisten with asphalt here remain in their primeval innocence. It's not so bad, really. It's nowhere near the hardship they must believe it is who each spring ask me, "How's your mud?" as they might ask poor Quasimodo, "How's your hump?" or the Ancient Mariner, "How's your albatross?"

AN ill-favored back road in April is the devil's railroad yard, and the devil is a rough switchman. Rounding a bend in a dirt road, you see before you an obscene snarl of mud ruts, some of them more than hubcap deep, black, sticky, bottomless — and lying in a hellish tangle that suggests Dante's tortured dream of the track yards back of North Station following an earthquake. Enter the bad patch, and the ruts seize your vehicle and fling it back and forth, wrenching the wheel, throwing you about inside like a shuttle, forcing creaks and snaps from the structure of your car, banging and scrubbing its undercarriage brutally against the road. The experience is the equivalent of shooting whitewater rapids in a handcar.

It ought to be possible to negotiate ruts in a muddy road just as you'd ride the rails: pick a set of ruts that are the same distance apart as the wheels of your car and simply tool along. In fact, that never works. The rut your car is in will heave you out and into the next rut, which will try to hurl your car clean off the road and into the ditch. A friend of mine has the explanation. "They move, you know," he says. "The ruts. No matter how you steer, the ruts move around and get you."

Of course. The ruts move. That's why you can't avoid them. There is an intelligence at work here. Far below, in the netherworld, a goatish figure takes the switch lever in its cloven hoof. The ruts shift, and you slew wildly across the road once again, bouncing helplessly among the black gullies. The devil is behind it, after all. Is it any wonder? Is it any surprise that the Prince of the Air should be drawing a railroad pension just like so many other elderly gentlemen in the country of the old Boston & Maine?

ONE day a couple of years ago, I set out to drive down the hill to the village at a moment when the town crew had lately passed my house grading and evening out the holes, bumps, and ruts that appear in the road each spring. All was well until I got to the steep pitch a mile from home. There my rear end slipped east in the smooth mud while my front slipped west, and the whole rig slithered toward the ditch like a pig at a party, arriving there in the twinkling of an eye. My neighbor pulled me out. As he unhitched his chain, he said to me, "You ought to know better than to try to drive on a road that's been fixed."

Wait, now. That's why we fix them, isn't it? The roads? So you can drive on them? Assuredly it is. But the way they go about mending the roads has a curious progression to it, a kind of dialectic that demands suffering and entails deep lessons about the life of man. As nearly as I can tell, to fix a bumpy, rutted road in mud season, you first scrape its surface into an impassable hogback of dirt, mud, and rocks. This ridge you grade down, spreading it across the road and making sure all the biggest rocks, which had migrated to the shoulders, have been put back in the middle. Finally you return with an enormous rake that evens out the top of the road, perking up those big rocks and stirring the surface into a kind of slurry: smooth, pretty, and for a while, as slick as any ice.

Roads, then, are like ourselves in this: getting fixed is no straight line. There is no royal road to virtue; you must wander through the thorns and thickets. You must enter the dark wood. To become well, you must be made ill; to be right, wrong. Have faith, but take it easy at first.

Games

WITHIN a couple of weeks after the new year turns the spring equinox, my bailiwick is ready to be visited by two of New England's most cherished institutions: mud and baseball. In my league, where most of the players are under fifteen and most of the salaries under seven figures, the two go very much together. My children's school digs out the bats and the softballs as soon as the snow is two-thirds gone. Therefore, spring training gets conducted in conditions some players would find inappropriate.

It's cold work, for one thing. The field is wet and the water that saturates it turns to ice at night. Balls hit sharply on the ground splash through the infield like ducks taking off from a pond. By the second inning, the players, the dog, and the fans are as muddy as plow horses. Few mud-time games go the full nine; you can't play well when you can't feel your fingers or feet for cold. We have had more than one game called on account of snow.

I pitch. I chase balls that come near where I am. Balls hit into the outfield, balls hit over the wall into the old pasture, balls hit beyond the house must be chased by the batter, after the dog loses interest. Those are the rules. They exist because I am a bit older than the other players and baseball is not really my game. At the Pastime I'm as good as I'm ever going to be, whereas the other players each year throw farther, hit harder, run faster. I have noticed that the annual advent of baseball at this changing time of the year seems to gain on me faster than it does on the rest of the squad. Their muscles, their minds switch into spring instantly on the day the bats and balls come out. Mine take longer.

No W blooming profusely in orange, red, and yellow on dark, bushy foliage and covering the garden with its strange perfume, the marigold comes into its own. It's not the most prettily scented flower, I know, but still the marigold is a favorite of mine precisely for its odor, a heavy autumnal reek of oranges and smoke that is unique in nature as far as I know, and that is as indispensable a part of the late-season garden as pumpkins and nodding sunflowers.

The pungent marigold I'm describing *(Tagetes),* an annual member of the daisy family, is a classic study in the naming of familiar plants, being called the African or French marigold when it is neither African nor French nor a marigold. The true marigold is *Calendula,* an old Eurasian medicinal sometimes called pot marigold. *Tagetes* is a New World plant that came to Europe around 1520 when Cortés, the conqueror of Mexico, sent its seeds back to Spain. The Aztecs had held the flower sacred and had even succeeded in producing hybrid plants with outsized flower heads. *Tagetes* came to the American colonies in the 1780s from nurseries in England and the Netherlands and must today be one of our commonest flowers.

Not everybody likes the marigold's musky scent. W. A. Burpee (1858–1915) set out to develop an odorless strain, finally succeeding by growing hybrids of a wild marigold from China. These are curiosities, however. The marigold's scent is an important part of its role in the garden as a repellent of insects. For my part, I plant marigolds because it's so easy — the seeds like little porcupine quills spring up in a couple of days — and because of that unmistakable smell that comes just before the first V of geese overhead to tell of the turning of the year.

IN the Greek myth the hero kills a dragon and sows its teeth in the earth. Immediately there sprouts up from each planted tooth an armed warrior. As the hero watches, spears, helmets, and swords break the earth and grow up before him.

Mushrooms appear in the pine woods in August with the mystery and suddenness of the soldiers of the dragon's teeth. In the speed with which they spring up, in their numbers, and in their strangeness, mushrooms are the offspring of the forest earth itself. One day the woods are dark, green, empty. Next morning they're full of pallid little visitors.

Like the soldiers in the myth, mushrooms have an air of threat, in part because some are known to be poisonous if eaten, but more, I think, because they are so odd, so unlike other vegetation. Mushrooms almost seem closer to animals or men than they are to plants. Their colors are not plant colors: livid white, gray, yellow, red, orange, the colors of fur, the colors of clothing. Their habit, too, is human. They appear overnight beneath the dark pines, where no plant will grow; and they spring up so quickly, thrusting aside the litter, pushing it up to — what? Not the sun. They have simple, human shapes: the straight, stout stalk; the head; the upright growth. But they're still, like painted dolls hidden among the rocks and roots.

I don't know the names of many mushrooms. One of my favorites turns up each August bearing on its head a neat coolie's hat of matted, tangled pine needles that it ripped from the earth and bore quickly up as it grew. I can imagine a mouse who fell asleep on the ground one night and woke the next morning to find herself hoisted into the air on the heads of a guard of little soldiers who carried her there like a bewildered queen and wouldn't put her down.

IN July, the bee balm, a native wildflower of the damp woodlands and streamsides, long since domesticated, educated, blooms
in the garden. It blooms in the most extraordinary fiery red, an
almost fierce color that doesn't seem to belong on a plant at all.
The flower is rough and shaggy. It looks like a rag doll, and as
the season wears on and the flower drops petals and parts and
begins to be somewhat raffish, like a rag doll it looks better and
better. Hummingbirds love the bee balm, and so do the monarch butterflies, which appear in numbers around the same
time the flower does. No doubt the bees love it too.

The bee balm *(Monarda didyma)*, a member of the mint family,
has a long and proud history, traceable through its several names.
It was imported from North America to England before 1745 by
the botanist John Bartram and became a favorite in the great
flower market at Covent Garden, London. The British called it
scarlet bergamot, because they believed the plant's aromatic
leaves and stems smelled like a popular orange of the day which
had come to England from the Italian city of Bergamo, north of
Milan. In the Colonies the plant was called Oswego tea, for it
was said the settlers and Indians around Oswego, New York,
drank an infusion of the leaves. Perhaps there was some ridicule
in a metropolitan, tea-drinking society's calling this American
wildling by that name. Oswego was a fort on the south shore of
Lake Ontario, founded as early as 1722. It was a wilderness
outpost at the back of beyond. To call *M. didyma* Oswego tea was
to say it was what passed for tea at places like Oswego, as we might
call crude oil Texas tea, or homemade whiskey Tennessee tea.

Games

FLEA markets are open for business about this time of year: the unimportant stuff of others' lives is on display for us all. I have always found fun and encouragement in flea markets, and it's evident that many find the same. I think the appeal of flea markets is to those who don't quite buy the idea of progress, those who persist in believing, even if they know better, that the old days — including fairly recent old days — were better days than our own. Flea markets allow these sentimental individuals to see, handle, enjoy, and even possess articles from the past, and so to partake in that past. The wealth of bent scythes, busted harnesses, rusty pails, anvils, liniment bottles, potato mashers, cracker tins, and the rest confirm a time when life was a bit tougher, but, some think, easier, too. When we commune with these articles at a flea market, we participate in that time through its humble appurtenances.

Flea market customers accept the genial fiction that because flea market items are for sale, they must have value. Flea market vendors, if they know better, don't dissent. There is an old story, perhaps apocryphal, of a Vermont flea market seller who died and went to hell. In punishment for his having presumed to charge real money for the junk he had sold every summer weekend for thirty years, the seller was condemned to pay ghostly visits to houses all across the land, retrieving the thousands of articles he had sold and refunding their prices. A collector in Akron wondered who could have entered his house by night, taken his old Prince Albert tobacco can, and left two bucks. The phantom flea marketer is still at large. Let other sellers ponder this tale as they spread their innocent wares on tables under June's warm sun.

IN August the butternut fall begins where I live, providing food for rodents. For people, the large nuts, which lie in the grass like green golf balls, furnish a kind of welcome wild candy, but they are also hazards to travel and to lawn care. Trod on, a butternut can turn your ankle. Run over with the lawn mower, the nuts can make an alarming racket rather like what would result from dropping a handful of nails and bolts into a kitchen blender. Of course you can plod about the yard to pick the butternuts up and cart them away, but that is idiot work. You can also ignore them and let the squirrels gather them for you, but that's too easy for most of us. Sitting back and letting nature do our work for us is not the way we Americans got where we are today. We constantly seek a better way, even to dispose of butternuts.

Last summer I discovered a heavy fall of fresh butternuts in the yard on a day when a kid happened to have left a plastic whiffle baseball bat lying handy. Immediately I thought of ball-players nonchalantly hitting fungoes into the outfield before a game. You know: you hold the bat at your shoulder with one hand, then toss the ball up in the air with your other hand, grab the bat, and cream the ball as it falls. I used to think of myself as being pretty good at that. I tried it with my butternuts, and the results were most satisfactory. I clean missed the first nut, but the next one I socked. It took off like a bird and landed in the meadow an impressive distance away. I find I can drive a butternut about eighty feet, which takes it well off my lawn. Now every evening I go out after supper and hit fifteen or twenty. In a week the lawn is as clear of butternuts as it needs to be, and I have honored what was the major sport of my childhood.

N O W, midway through the hot summer days, the fishing is as bad as it gets. You might as well try to pull a brook trout out of a bowl of soup. And yet the fishermen seem to be at it as actively as ever, whipping away at the streams and plunking in the ponds — and not just the kids who don't know any better, but more experienced fishermen as well. They're out there, too, though the water is dead and the fish all asleep. Why? Why do they persist? Maybe the answer is in the observation of a trout fisherman I know who found that he was becoming more interested in the bugs, larvae, and nymphs that he imitated to catch fish than he was in the fish themselves. He and the other dog days fishermen are practicing their art for reasons that have nothing to do with fish but everything to do with fishing.

What is behind the tendency in fishing — indeed, in so many of man's activities — for attention, affection, to shift from the object of pursuit to the pursuit itself? Method becomes as important as result, more important. Method becomes *style*. What difference does it make whether you kill your trout with a dry fly, or with a plastic worm, or with a real worm, or with a stick of dynamite? The last method is the best in that it procures the most fish with the least effort, but it doesn't admit of stylish execution, of perfection aspired to, as fly fishing does. What is style, then? Is there a hidden inevitability in man's affairs, a kind of dialectic in our experience, that drives us to learn to inquire about the game and ignore its purpose? What would that mean, for example, in law, in politics? Or is it just that every occupation exists only as it is engaged in by individuals, and individuals grow older, and style is an old man's business?

IN a well-stocked fishing shop today the casual buyer is lost. A veritable Louvre of baits is exhibited to his bewildered senses. Time was, you could go to work with a plug that looked like a fishing lure ought to look: a red-headed torpedo with big googly eyes and two sets of huge hooks that would have done for a plesiosaur.

No more. You need an engineering degree at least to equip yourself for fishing today. The wall of the fishing shop is stacked to the ceiling with lures. The old bass plug was made of pine wood and covered with boat paint. Modern lures are made of every known material *except* wood. There are lures of steel, tin, brass, aluminum, epoxy, fiberglass, rubber, and five hundred different kinds of plastic. There are lures in every color and in every combination of colors. There are lures that imitate living things like worms, frogs, mice, bugs, baby muskrats, and fish; and there are lures that imitate nothing — or, not nothing, but *other fishing lures.* What else are we to make of a spoon that's half a foot long and takes two men to cast? There are lures that swim and lures that splash, and there are lures that make little beeping sounds that are supposed to attract fish.

To attract fish, did you say? That's part of the program, certainly, but it's only part. There is another term in the system that relates the fish to the fishing shop, and that term is the fisherman. Those fancy lures don't catch fish on the shelves. Before they can hook a fish they must hook a fisherman, and there is the point of the profusion of styles, materials, colors, and sizes of lure. The fish were just as happy with the old bass plug. They don't care. It's the owners of the fishing shops who have seen the light, just as saints Peter and Andrew did beside the Sea of Galilee in the gospel. "Follow me," the Lord said unto them, "and I will make you fishers of men."

PEOPLE in the retail business will tell you that the three secrets of keeping store are location, location, and location. But if you're a young entrepreneur just starting out, and if your premises are at all rural, you may have to learn the importance of location the hard way. The young entrepreneur I'm thinking of was six last August. Finding herself short of funds and wanting to celebrate summer by shining up one of the icons of American childhood, she decided to open a lemonade stand beside the road she lived on. The lemonade she made, with a little help in directing the sugar toward the pitcher. A card table, paper cups, ice, a sign, a money box, and the elements of commerce seemed all to be in place. Tuesday morning right after breakfast she opened for business. Nickel a cup was the price.

Location was not long in delivering its stern verdict. The road her stand served, while not entirely void of traffic, was about a four- or five-car-per-hour road on a Tuesday morning. The cars that did pass tended to be the same ones, moreover, and their drivers tended not to be thirsty. They'd wave, but they wouldn't buy. Beer crowd, I guess. In any case, business was unbrisk. I bought a cup, and I stood the house one; but although my money was good, I'm a close relative of the proprietor, so my trade was not too important.

"Bit slow," I remarked.

"I'm never going to make any money," the proprietor said.

"Cheer up," I said. "Maybe a bus will come along and you'll sell it all at once."

"Buses never come along," she said. I bought another cup.

"Can you watch for a while?" she asked.

"Me?" I said.

And so another small business became a statistic.

Trees Alive & Dead

THE ancients of the Mediterranean world are supposed to have gotten the idea for their monumental building style from the woodlands and sacred groves of their countryside. The serene columns of the Parthenon are forest trees expressed in stone: the marble shaft is the tree's trunk, and the column's capital, in its variety of designs, the leaves and branches. If so, the tree that inspired antiquity must, I think, have been the beech, for it grows in the Old World as well as the New, and it is preeminently a tree that looks like architecture.

In my territory the beech *(Fagus grandifolia)* is a tree of the uplands rather than the valleys. In the hardwood hills it frequently takes over small patches of forest in which no other tree grows. These beech groves are where you can best see the curious architectural quality of the tree. Its trunk is unique: straight, smooth even in old trees, and a pale blue-gray, the color of smoke, the color of stone. The main branches in a woodland tree begin at some height, and so in a beech wood you seem to be walking among aisles of uniform columns that support a roof, just as in a temple. It's not hard to imagine that the look of such a wood might have given rise to the classical temple style.

Well, if this brief excursion into the history of world religion is on the speculative side, there is no doubt that the animals and birds would worship in the beech woods if they could, for many live by them. Woodland animals from the bear to the mouse take the autumn crop of beechnuts as the main part of their diet. Beech mast is the bread of the woods for wildlife, and so these groves are the forest's bakery, whether or not they are its church.

SURROUNDING my fenceless little vegetable garden are eight old posts indicating the line the fence took when the garden was bigger than it is today. Rusty nails and scraps of hex netting adorn these posts. They are gray, rough, cracked. None of them stands up straight. They all lean this way and that, giving the property a look of ramshackle decay, as though the posts were ancient villagers, idle, disreputable, who sit all day in front of the store cackling at the follies of the industrious.

The garden posts are of different sizes. The top of the tallest must be nine feet off the ground, the shortest is the height of my shoulder. They're round, mostly six or seven inches thick. The fattest has a knothole where chickadees sometimes nest. The posts are made of black locust trunks, and unless I cut them up and burn them, they're here to stay. They held the remains of the garden fence when we came here twenty years ago, and they're visible in photos of the place taken twenty years before that. There used to be nine posts. I uprooted one of them and moved it into the cellar to brace a broken floor joist. When I dug that post up, I found its buried third, at least thirty-five years in the earth, as sound as the section that was exposed. Locust posts set in the ground by the first colonists at Jamestown, Virginia, in 1607, were as good as new a hundred years later.

Nothing that endures as long as these posts can be entirely good-natured. Try driving a fence staple into one of them. You might as well hammer a strand of cooked spaghetti into a steel girder. Best leave the posts to their retirement; let the beans climb up them, let the flycatcher in the long summer evening find atop the tallest its lofty perch.

JUNE 1993

The Lives of Animals

To this observer, evolution seems to be a process that is far from stern, far from having the solemnity becoming a fundamental principle of life on earth. Rather, the profusion of forms of plants and animals, the variety and cleverness of their behavior, the fullness and complexity with which earth, air, and water are packed with life — all these seem to belong to an evolution that is always experimenting, improvising, being playful. The origin of species is something like a game, and in my neighborhood one of its best sports is the creature called the flying squirrel *(Glaucomys volans)*. This is an otherwise rather dumpy, stubby little rodent that has, for no good reason, wings. It's as though nature gave the squirrel wings casually, for fun, with the randomness of a bright child drawing horns and mustachios on people in magazines to make a rainy afternoon pass. Let's see what this guy looks like with an elephant nose. Let's make this one fly.

The flying squirrels are abroad on summer nights. They're the size of a big red squirrel; they have fine, fancy gray fur, enormous liquid eyes, and long flaps of loose skin that run between their fore- and hindquarters on each side. They extend these flaps like sails to fly. When the squirrel is at rest, the folds of soft, furred skin lie opulently around its shoulders. It's fur that looks as though it belongs inside the deepest Cadillac on Park Avenue.

All the books agree that the flying squirrel can't really fly. It only glides, falling on its wide sails, the experts insist. Ignore them. The experts are jealous, that's all. If you or I could jump out of a tall tree and float for a hundred feet, sometimes carrying the kids with us; if we could in the process turn, stall, even gain a bit of altitude, as the flying squirrel can, would we hesitate to call it flight?

THERE is a good old New England story about a village somewhere in Connecticut that was overrun by frogs one summer night. Frogs by the tens of thousands marshaled outside the village and advanced in assault formation, briefly occupying the settlement and forcing the people to take refuge in their homes behind barricaded doors. This happened long ago, perhaps in the eighteenth century during the French and Indian Wars. In truth, there are still people who don't believe it happened at all; but even assuming that the story isn't strictly fact, it's easy to guess at its origin in the leaping profusion of little frogs that throng the grass as summer reaches its height.

They are common leopard frogs *(Rana pipiens)*, green or brown with brown spots that I guess make them look about as much like a leopard as a frog can look. They are everywhere in the grass in July, in meadows and lawns, and by gardens. With every step you take, another one flings out before you, a slick dark streak through the grass (almost as though the grass itself has taken quick, startling motion), bounding away on sleek legs that for strength and skill must be the envy of any dancer.

The frogs that pop out from everywhere in July and August are little things, not much bigger than a man's thumb. They are young, seemingly; they come from this spring's eggs and polliwogs in the wet ditches, puddles, and brooks. After midsummer they are on the move, and a curious thing about these frogs is that they stray so far from water, much farther than most other frogs, which are practically aquatic animals. Maybe the leopard frog represents the advance guard of frog evolution, separating itself from water more than its cousins, preparing for a fully terrestrial life. It took a pretty modern frog to drive a whole town behind its shutters that night.

JULY 1984

NEAT little piles of nutshells and scales from the cones of pines and hemlocks in the woods are the work of the red squirrel, a creature of habit, which likes to return with its forage to the same place to eat. This is the small, white-bellied squirrel with the white eye ring and russet back and flanks that is so at home in the trees and makes such a racket in the summer woods.

The red squirrel *(Tamiasciurus hudsonicus)* is exclusively an inhabitant of the northern forests, for its diet depends on the seeds of cone-bearing trees. It's common in its range, but it is a shy, alert, and solitary animal that doesn't tolerate the approach of people or pets, and it never goes far from the trees. The red squirrel's ability to get around high among the branches is extraordinary. On an individual's home range, which may be as little as a few acres in extent, each squirrel seems to have established routes leading from branch to branch and from tree to tree, and it travels them — on perilous twigs seventy-five feet above the ground — with complete and careless ease. It's less well known that red squirrels are good swimmers. They have been found far out on big lakes, including Lake Champlain, where one was seen swimming strongly more than a mile from shore.

Red squirrels nest in the trees, but they store nuts, seeds, and other food in holes in the ground. Other squirrels hide nuts singly here and there and then apparently forget about them, but the red squirrel makes true collections or caches of food, which it uses as stores. This squirrel is also supposed to be especially intelligent about selecting its food. It is said that a red squirrel can tell unerringly whether a nut is sound or bad and that no red squirrel will ever store or try to open an empty nut.

LATE one night I looked up for some reason from my book and saw, watching me from a corner across the room, a little mouse. I looked at the mouse, and the mouse looked at me, for the space of maybe three minutes. Then it began poking along the baseboard, keeping close to the wall. At that moment the dog stirred in her sleep, and the mouse retired behind a cabinet. Later, on my way to bed, I peeped in back there, but it was gone. A mouse from the woods, that one had been — not one of the gray house mice or the stubby brown field voles that make up the bulk of the local rodentry, but a delicate creature with a russet brown back and a pure white belly, the colors of a springtime deer.

The white-footed mouse *(Peromyscus leucopus)* lives mainly in the brushy woods and edges of the pine-and-hardwood uplands. The old stone walls, thickets, and decaying stumps of those woods might have been designed as the home of a species that, as the prey of every carnivore that walks, flies, or crawls, must live by keeping close to cover rather than, say, by outbreeding the opposition in the manner of the voles, which frequent open places.

These mice are nocturnal creatures and live on seeds and nuts, insects, sometimes carrion. They are assiduous savers of food, caching seeds and other forage. In the winter you never see the white-foot, although you find its light, hopping footprints laid like a lace ribbon over the snow. In the summer the mouse may wander into barns and houses, as did the one that visited me. Indoors the white-footed mouse seems strangely calm, less frightened than a house mouse. It sits quietly and watches you with its wide, shining eyes as black as onyx, as though it were admiring you at the same time you admired it.

GLIDING off the edge of an old stone wellhead with the bewildering motion peculiar to its kind, the garter snake pours itself into the grass and disappears. It is gone in the same instant that it is seen. And for that instant, however well I know the innocence of the harmless creature, however many of them I have myself kept and handled, I pull back. The irreducible creepiness of the snake is not in its crawling over the ground or in the evil reputation of some of its tribe, but in the uncanniness of its way of going: the snake moves without moving.

Our familiar snake is *Thamnophis sirtalis sirtalis,* the eastern garter. It lives among the stone walls, by the house foundations, beside the gardens. A big one is a foot and a half long. One summer we kept a little one in a dry fish tank. Every week or so it ate an earthworm. The great American herpetologist Ditmars had several garter snakes that he kept in his study. "They seemed to have real affection," he wrote, "and enjoyed being handled." I can't say I ever felt burdened by the affection of our little snake, which the children named Slithers (Slith for short). At the end of the summer we let him (her?) go because we weren't sure we could keep her (him?) healthy over winter. If Slithers's affectionate nature was injured by our releasing him, he didn't let his feelings show much at all.

A garter snake can live for ten years or more. Today when I spot one and can catch it, I examine it closely and wonder if it's old Slith. Sometimes I think I detect in the snake an answering nod, a faint smile of old affection. But I'm never sure: it's been too many years, and the fact is, all those snakes smile about the same.

THE first box turtle I ever saw was eating raspberries in a meadow in Pennsylvania. I have since found others in Connecticut and one high above Lake Shore Drive, Chicago. The last was a little out of its usual setting, no doubt, but it seemed happy to be there as far as anyone could tell.

A well-grown box turtle *(Terrapene carolina carolina)* is eight or nine inches long overall, with a bright, ruby red eye and an ornate shell, high-domed and marked with broad, symmetrical yellow or orange splotches on a black ground. Often the central markings look like a capital E, but the pattern is variable; no two turtles look exactly alike. The undershell, or plastron, is hinged a third of the way back from the front end. The box turtle can draw itself into its shell and close the hinged plastron like a lid — hence its name. Indians in Florida, who believed this turtle to have great power, took its behavior as a weather sign: if a box turtle kept to its shell and refused to emerge, the weather would be dry; if it was active, rain would come.

The box turtle has the distinction of being the longest-lived reptile in North America. One individual lived to be 138. They inhabit dry woods all over the northeastern states, subsisting on berries, shoots, insects, and earthworms. In the fall they dig themselves into the ground and hibernate. They make good companions. My mother knew a lady who kept a box turtle as a pet in a fairly flossy apartment building in Chicago. She fed it lettuce, a little raw hamburger. In the autumn, when the turtle looked ready to hibernate, she stuck it in a hatbox from Marshall Field's and put it on a closet shelf. In the spring she brought it out along with the golf clubs and the tennis rackets.

SECRET agents, undercover cops, and young women in night-gowns aren't the only ones who can have Hollywood adventures, action-movie escapes. The humblest rodent can tell of catastrophes.

Late one night, investigating a faint sound that came from the kitchen closet, I found a mouse trapped in a glass bottle up on a high shelf. It was a deer mouse, an outdoor creature usually, and a great gatherer of seeds and nuts. The bottle was a clean, empty quart that had once held fancy vinegar. The mouse had evidently discovered our supply of birdseed and had hit on the plan of dropping sunflower seeds into the bottle for safekeeping. An elegant scheme, but at last the mouse perceived what others have learned in dealings with institutions of safekeeping: putting in is easy; taking out, not always so easy. With the bottle a quarter full of seeds, the mouse must have decided to visit its assets. Once in there, it couldn't get out.

I took the bottle down from the shelf. I wouldn't have hurt the mouse, but as I held it in its bottle, it looked up at me the way Fay Wray, atop the Empire State Building, looked at that big gorilla. I laid the bottle on its side in the closet and left it, so the mouse could walk out. Half an hour later it was still there. It couldn't or wouldn't leave. I could think of only one solution — a crash. I took the bottle outside, tilted it so seeds and mouse slid toward the neck, and gave its base a smart rap with a hammer. Nothing. Again. An explosion of glass, seeds, and escaping mouse. Sweeping up, I wondered what in the world he would tell his friends, what tale of Jules Verne out of Ian Fleming. Where would he begin?

AMONG the complex lives of the common creatures around our houses and gardens, none makes a richer narrative than that of the red eft *(Notophthalmus viridescens viridescens)*. The career of this two-inch salamander is like an old-fashioned novel, full of change and shifting identities, full, above all, of journeying. Born in a pond or brook, the eft begins its active life as a quarter-inch larva, green and legless. It lives in the water during its first summer, then in the fall the mature eft leaves its native pond and goes forth on dry land to seek its fortune. It has taken on a brilliant orange color with ruby spots.

The eft lives in the moist woods and thickets. It feeds mostly on insects and earthworms. Not a bad life, probably, but the eft's journey is far from over. It remains on land for two or three years, then makes its way back to water. There it changes color again, to an olive green, and becomes fully aquatic once more. Now it's no longer an eft but a newt — same animal, different name, as though the eft had been elevated to the peerage. Back in the water it lives out its life as a newt, and in the water it reproduces, making little efts who will have the same adventures.

A curious thing about the eft is its sudden energy. I once found one hiding beneath the pea vines. It didn't run away. It seemed a slow creature. But I happened to turn it over, and it instantly flipped itself back onto its feet. I tried again with the same result. I could not put the little thing on its back; it snapped right-side up more quickly than my eye could follow. I suppose I shouldn't have been surprised. The young heroes of Fielding and Smollett, too, are always nimble.

LACKING science, animals seem to have a kind of physical, or cellular, intelligence that ought to be as miraculous to us as our human learning might be to them. We have instruments and measurements. They have senses — many more and better, perhaps, than five. We have logic; they have repose. We know; they act. Our different ways of living in the same world are well demonstrated by the different ways in which we accept the seasons.

People take the seasons as they come, one at a time. They understand the seasons, foresee them, plan for them. Animals — or, anyway, the ones we're pleased to call the higher animals — seem in some way to live in all the seasons at once, all the time. Or at least they experience the seasons as overlapping to a far greater degree than we do. I'm thinking of a particular cat, a well-grown black male named, with more affection than originality, Puss. Like most cats, Puss likes to get around. All spring and summer he checks in each morning to eat, then immediately runs back outdoors.

Sometime in August, though, Puss makes a slight adjustment in his routine. Now, in the morning after breakfast, instead of heading right back out, he goes upstairs to one of the beds and sleeps for two hours. Then he's off again. At this time, you understand, we're not far past midsummer. It's hot, green, dusty. The days are long, the nights full of fun. And yet Puss forgoes a measure of it all for the sake of a nap. Why? I think because some deep sense warns him of the distant approach of the indoor season, winter, a matter of which he knows nothing, or anyway not as we reckon knowing. In the middle of the endless summer, and for reasons no reason knows, he is preparing his complex life for another world.

Big Weather

A COUPLE of summers ago we lost a fairly large tree to a euphemism. We were lucky. The same euphemism did a good deal of damage in the river valley. A barn was destroyed, and many trees were down. The culprit was one of the very strong, very local summer storms that blow through here every few years, storms that have, in this part of the country at least, an odd kind of unreality.

Other regions are more forthright. Consider the weather in question: the sky grows darker and darker until the afternoon is as black and still as the inside of an ink bottle. Suddenly the wind begins to blow violently, a terrible thrashing, screaming wind that seems to come from all directions at once and brings sheets of rain or hail — and then abruptly stops. Trees are uprooted, roofs torn off, cars tossed about, but with an ominous capriciousness: one house will be wrecked, the house next door will be untouched.

In the Midwest, where I grew up, they know what to call these storms. They're tornadoes. But everybody knows New England doesn't have tornadoes, and so when one of these rippers occurs in Vermont, it's called a "storm front," a "squall line," or some such, in a triumph of euphemism over experience.

Maybe the storms I've tried to describe aren't true tornadoes from the point of view of science. (They lack the famous funnel cloud, for one thing.) But that's not much consolation to the fellow who lost his barn, who might well recall a bit of wisdom that was current a few years back down in Washington, D.C., a town where they know a thing or two about destructive wind: if it looks like a duck, and it walks like a duck, and it quacks like a duck — it may be a duck.

WE are aware of the weather in more ways than we know. Of course, we are informed about it by the news and by our friends and neighbors, and we observe it immediately when we look out the window. But our senses and minds are alert also to weather signals far more subtle than a local report or the sound of rain on a roof. Perhaps these more obscure clues are most easily observed when they tell of extreme weather, especially extreme weather at some distance.

It will be just two years ago this month that Hurricane Hugo emerged from the Atlantic's great autumnal storm factory below the Tropic of Cancer. It raged over the Leeward Islands and hit the Carolina coast as one of the most powerful and dangerous hurricanes in recent years. Hugo didn't have a lot of punch left for New England, fortunately, but we felt the breeze from the swing he took at South Carolina — not a mighty blast, but a passing flick that was the more ominous for having its full force withheld.

The day Hugo was ripping around down south, the air at my house, a little less than a thousand miles to the north, was full of unease. The sky was a funny purple-gray, and there was a wind — never a very strong wind — that was unusual in that it came from the south and east, a rare thing here where the winds are northwesterly. More disquieting, the wind was steady rather than gusting. Hugo's wind leaned into the trees with a constant pressure, steadily bending them like bows rather than making them whip and thrash their tops as an ordinary wind would do. Those gently bending trees and that south wind were what set my senses on edge until the great storm scattered and died out.

The Minds of Birds

BIRDS don't talk anymore, it seems. They used to. Not too long ago many birds could talk, and some were positively eloquent. "Teacher, teacher," birds used to say, and "Take a drink," and "Poor Will." More talkative birds in those days said, "Who cooks for you all?" and (my favorite) "O Canada, Canada."

Today the discourse of the birds has gone to hell. Any bird guide published in the last few years will show how diminished are their abilities as speakers. Where they used to say, "Take a drink" and "Poor Will," most birds now, it seems, are content with *tchep* and *dee dee dee*. And what now passes for bird eloquence? *Teedle teedle*, and *chupety swee-ditchety*.

What happened? Have the birds' schools failed in rigor and produced a generation of dummies, as we are told our own human schools have? No: the reason the birds can't talk anymore is that we won't let them. Our forebears were delighted, they were relieved, to find in an enormous and scary wilderness harmless creatures that seemed to call to them in words they could recognize. They piled "Teacher, teacher" on "Poor Will" and soon had a complete chorus of birds who spoke the language of the farm, the village, the woods. That chorus we now prefer to break up. No ornithologist today will allow a bird that says, "O Canada, Canada." To recognize such a call would be to proceed as if animals were like people — it would be to *anthropomorphize*. That is a dirty word. It goes with a whole way of thinking about nature that is archaic, sentimental, and unscientific. Birds can't talk.

There is a bird around my place that sits up in the grape tangle, wasting time, while I am sitting on the grass, wasting time. The bird knows, and I know, that it's June. The bird says, "Gather ye rosebuds while ye may."

WOODPECKERS as a family must know something of
Original Sin, as other birds do not; for woodpeckers are, preeminently, birds that eat their bread in the sweat of their faces.
Not that it's easy being a flycatcher, say, or a heron or a finch —
but the bugs, frogs, and seeds that make the food of those
fortunate species are pretty much there for the taking, aren't
they? All those birds have to do is be in the right place at the
right time. The woodpecker must dig and delve and work for his
living. If you have watched one toiling over a tree branch, you
know that wood*pecker* is a bad name, suggesting a way of forag-
ing more fastidious and less intense than the actions the bird
really performs to get its food. You might as well call an open-
heart surgeon a "chest pecker." The woodpecker drives his beak
into the bark and twists, rips, gouges, scrapes, yanks, and digs.
He moves wood. The big pileated woodpeckers around here
leave at the foot of a tree a pile of chips that would make an
axman proud. Their smaller friends, the hairy and downy woodpeckers, make less of a mess but are equally assiduous. These
birds know that in this world you have to hustle. They go after a
tree hammer and tongs; they don't expect lunch simply to wander by.

Woodpeckers make other birds look like triflers. Their lives
have a complexity and purpose that remind us of ourselves.
They work because they must, and so do we; and neither of us
complains. We both get along. But life is unfair. And when a
dilettante phoebe floats by a woodpecker's branch, you can see
the latter glance up briefly, a little crossly, and then return to his
work, like a cobbler looking out the window of his humble shop
at the passing of a brougham.

Bugs & Butterflies

S O M E O N E left a light burning in a window last night, and this morning a luna moth is clinging to the screen. It came out of the night woods, drawn by the lighted window, and now it rests motionless in the daylight, hardly stirring its wings when I touch them. With its size and its astonishing color, the moth *(Actias luna)* seems to have come from a different world. No other insect looks so out of place in New England's cold northern setting. The luna's wings, which can measure five inches from tip to tip, are the palest blue-green, the color of a Caribbean pool. Its wings have long, slender tails which trail like the feathers of a bright tropical bird. The front edges of its wings are purple or maroon, and its body is the whitest thing in nature.

Despite its exotic look, the luna is, as far as I can tell, about the commonest big moth in northern New England. Its larva, a fat, light green caterpillar the size of a man's thumb, feeds all summer on the leaves of hickories, oaks, butternuts, and cherry trees. It makes a rough silk cocoon among dry leaves on the ground in late summer and spends the winter under the snow as a pupa. In June the adult moths emerge from their cocoons, fly, mate, lay eggs, and die — all in the space of four or five days. Like the other large silk moths, the luna has no working mouth parts and so does not feed. Its brief life is devoted to mating and egg laying.

The moth has long been associated with the moon — hence its name, *luna* — although the origin of the association isn't clear. Henry David Thoreau speculated on the point when on June 27, 1859, he found one of the moths at the edge of a swamp near Concord, Massachusetts. The luna, he wrote, "has more relation to the Moon by its pale, hoary-green color and its sluggishness by day than by the form of its tail," which some old naturalists had thought resembled the crescent moon.

F R O M the long grass beside the garden comes the first tentative bleat of the field cricket *(Gryllus)*. In the late summer its note fills the afternoon, and when the nights first turn cold, a few crickets will move into the house, where one will speak now and then from the corner. Indoors or out, the cricket's chirp is a strangely elusive sound; it seems always to come from just to one side, as though each chirp were its own echo and not the chirp itself.

The echoing quality of the chirp may come from the way the sound is produced. The male cricket has on the underside of each forewing a heavy, toothed rib and, near it, a hard ridge. To chirp, he elevates his forewings and rubs them one over the other with a sidewise, hula movement that drags the ridge of the right wing over the toothed vein of the left, and vice versa, making a *zing* just as you would do by drawing your thumbnail along the teeth of a comb. The sound is amplified by the vibrating surface of the forewings. Since each wing has both sounding parts, each chirp is doubled, which perhaps helps account for its uncanny, sourceless nature.

A near relative of the field cricket is the tree cricket *(Oecanthus)*. The tree cricket is smaller than the field cricket and is green while the latter is black or brown. One tree cricket *(O. niveus)* is supposed to be a kind of living thermometer. If you count the number of chirps per minute, divide by four, and add thirty-seven, you will arrive at the temperature in degrees Fahrenheit. To me the truth of that proposition is less extraordinary than the fact that it is known. I mean, who figures this stuff out? What mathematics-obsessed countryman sat patiently in the woods with a thermometer and an adding machine, counting chirps?

J U N E is bug time. Every entry into the woods brings forth an attentive escort, zipping, hovering, whining, biting. Once again it is necessary to decide which is the most hateful of the Big Three of woodland tormentors: the mosquito, the black fly, or the deer fly. Those who know real wild country advance the claim of one of the first two, but I live in relatively settled parts, and there I'll hold out for the deer fly *(Chrysops)* as worst bug.

Deer flies are mostly buzzers, not biters. They like hair. A deer fly will buzz around your head, ears, and neck, persistently circling. I would rather have fifty of the local mosquitoes than one of these.

Deer flies are smarter than other insects. They work a path in the woods the way an expert undercover surveillance team works the streets of a city to keep watch on a suspect. You enter the woods, and Deer Fly No. 1 picks you up. It stays with you for twenty or thirty yards, buzzing and bothering. Then No. 1 fades out. You go on your way untormented for a few minutes. Deer Fly No. 2 picks you up, follows you for another leg. Then No. 2 falls away, and No. 3 takes you up. Where did they learn to do this?

There is one way in which deer flies are vulnerable. Since they work in relays, it is theoretically possible for you to break up their assault. Suppose, with a lucky blow, you get the individual who has you in charge. Now, the deer fly that came before the one you have just killed is out of the picture; it has passed you on. The next one hasn't come on shift. You're in the clear — as long as you remain exactly where you are. In three or four months the deer flies will be gone, and you will have bested them for sure.

IF we are to be invaded by alien monsters out of a 1950s creature feature, it will happen on a warm, soft summer night. Remember *Them!* (1954)? In that classic screamer the invaders were giant ants. They were frightening enough, too, but we have with us in real life a far scarier being that stalks the dark nights. The dobsonfly *(Corydalus cornutus)* is a nightmare union of dragonfly, crocodile, and helicopter. It's brown, has four narrow, transparent wings that may span four inches, a round head, and the vacant, incurious, protruding eyes of the movies' most threatening destroyers. The male dobsonfly has as well a huge pair of jaws that stick far out in front of its mouth like twin butcher's knives. It comes to night lights like a moth, flying with an ungainly whirligig action. By day it's sluggish, but if you poke it, it rears up its head like a cobra and shows you those prodigious choppers.

In fact, like many but maybe not all movie monsters, the dobsonfly is entirely harmless. It's one of the lacewings, more like a mayfly than a dragon. It takes its name from its larval form, carnivorous creatures called dobsons that live in fresh water. That larva is a considerably more formidable animal than the fly it becomes. One encyclopedia calls it a "ferocious predator" of small aquatic life. It's a long, jointed crawler that looks like a caterpillar. Fishermen know the dobson as the hellgrammite; it's said to be death on bass. Its adult form, the dobsonfly, is death on nothing, despite its menacing aspect. The main mystery about it for me is, Who was the Dobson who gave his name to the larva and hence the fly? I'd like to think he was in the cast of *Them!,* but the name apparently goes back to 1889.

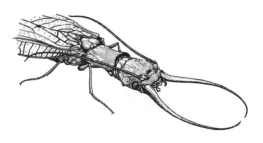

ONE day a couple of summers ago I came upon a troop of large black ants crawling in single file up a tall grass stem in a meadow where I walked. There must have been fifty or more ants, and they proceeded slowly in tight formation, nose to tail, along the stalk. What happened when they reached the top? I don't know because I didn't wait to see. I was walking that day, not looking, and although I noted the ant procession as a remarkable thing, I passed on without learning more about it, consoling myself with the thought that, after all, there is probably not much that's new on ants. No doubt antologists have long since observed and understood such processions, however strange they are to me, an amateur of ants. Let the professionals look into these marching ants, I thought; they can figure the thing out better than I.

But what a lazy, unworthy notion it is, the idea that all the secrets of nature's everyday life have been discovered, that any purposeful investigation of nature can only be the domain of scientists, specialists, and others better trained than we. Can't science itself begin in curiosity, and isn't curiosity reborn in each of us and directed at even the humblest phenomena — until we decide that everything is known to science and give up our excitement at ordinary sights and sounds? Maybe we should begin to think of seeing nature as an art rather than a science. No one believes that the world's musicians, painters, authors have exhausted the subject matter of art to the point where there is no further need for music, painting, or literature. Can we renew our curiosity, and so our will to learn from what we see, by imagining that we go to the trees, stars, bugs, and grass as an artist to his work: intent, expectant, delighting?

FIREFLIES wander through the midsummer night. Their strange, cold little lights flash on and off as though they were trying to send signals in a code nobody knows but they. In fact, as I understand it, particular patterns of illumination in fireflies function to attract mates. Fireflies are looking for romance like everybody else, then; but I can't get over the idea that if only I knew how to interpret them, the winking, drifting lights would have something to say to me. Someday I'll get the fireflies' message. I hope it's not an ad.

The fact that there are little beetles flying around out there that can turn themselves on and off like a flashlight has always seemed to me to come right out of the book of miracles, but in truth creatures that light up are by no means rare. There are luminescent shrimp, jellyfish, squid, clams, snails, worms, and fish — lots of fish — as well as insects. Most are marine, however, perhaps the reason a landsman is so struck by the firefly, which occurs virtually everywhere.

Fireflies themselves may be any of several insects. The ones we see are beetles of the family *Lampyridae*, of which there are 140 different species in North America. Elsewhere in the world there are other, greater light-up bugs. Some are rich in legend. The best such story I know concerns the *cucujo (Pyrophorus)*, a large click beetle of Latin America. According to *The Conquest of Mexico*, it was this beetle, shining in the night, that gave the great Cortés a crucial victory over his enemy Narváez. The soldiers of the latter, besieged in the night by Cortés in one of the temples in the Aztec town of Cempoala (modern Veracruz province, Mexico), took the lights of the summer fireflies for the matches on the muskets of a vast army and surrendered to Cortés's force, which in fact was tiny. June 1520.

IT'S around the middle of August that the orange monarch butterflies begin to appear in numbers over the gardens, meadows, and roadsides. A monarch drifts across the yard, alights on a flower, leaves it, floats back the way it came, finds another flower, changes its mind and returns to the first, rests, then wanders on. Other butterflies may dart quickly here and there or move steadily ahead in a businesslike way; the monarch has an utterly languid, purposeless style of flight that never seems to take it much of anywhere. It lingers at every flower, turns in early every day, and travels only when the weather is fine. This butterfly has all the time in the world. Its summer flights are like the progress of a lady of leisure killing an afternoon at Bloomingdale's.

The loitering flight of this laziest of butterflies is in contrast to the prodigious journey it is embarked on. So far from being the idling Sunday sailor it appears, the monarch *(Danaus plexippus)* is the insect world's Magellan. Individuals born in Canada and the northern states migrate each year as far as Mexico, and monarchs have been found hundreds of miles out over the ocean. There are birds that travel farther, but no migrator — no bird, no insect, no animal — makes its trip with more nonchalance. It's a wonder the monarch gets as far as the next county, so lackadaisical is its motion, so readily does it break its voyage to stop at a flower. I can imagine the monarch finally arrives at its tropical destination with something of a surprise, as though our shopper, having left Bloomingdale's, just decided to pop into Bergdorf's for half an hour, then moved on down Fifth Avenue to Saks, and so on until she found herself in Acapulco.

"Oh, dear," she'd say.

THIS is the season of signs. The signs are that the summer will end, and of them all, the best and most eloquent is the ringing of the cicada, which comes down from all the trees. You will hear a thousand for every one you see, but I found one once on a windowsill. It's an insect that looks somehow like a fish: two inches long, black, with shiny green bars, bulging eyes, and big stiff wings clear as glass.

The cicada is called the weather bug, I guess because it appears and begins its strange calling now, when summer bends fairly toward the equinox, bringing changes and sudden rain. Its noise is hard to describe; there is nothing like it in nature that I have heard. Imagine a whine, the sound of a power saw going at high speed into a cracked board. You can't tell, when you hear the cicada, just where its whine comes from, for it seems to be everywhere, like air turned to sound.

The cicada's buzz continues through the warm afternoons. It is to be heard constantly, without interruption, as though nothing could disturb the insect or make it stop its song. Nothing can. The French entomologist J. H. Fabre was struck a hundred years ago by the persistence of the cicada's call in his village, Sérignan-du-Comtat, in the Vaucluse, north of Avignon. He tried to startle the cicadas, to make them shut up for a minute. Fabre banged on pans and blew horns under the trees where the cicadas whined. They didn't care. He went to the length of rolling a pair of cannon under the trees and firing blanks. The cicadas were oblivious. Nothing the naturalist did could interrupt their buzz, any more than he could have interrupted the seasons in their change, which the cicada appears to proclaim.

Change

AUGUST is a summer month in everybody's calendar, but there is a tree that knows better: the Judas tree. Every neighborhood has one — a hardwood that changes color weeks before its season. These are not unhealthy trees or trees too near the road, either of which may also yellow early. Judas trees are fine, well-grown specimens that are simply on an accelerated autumn schedule, and since everybody else's autumn inevitably catches up to theirs, they seem to be trees that know something.

There is such a tree a few miles from where I live, a sugar maple maybe sixty feet high, growing up on a bank above the river. Every year in the middle of August, over three or four days, it turns from green to scarlet. Every tree around it remains green, however, and for a month, until its neighbors begin to turn, this tree rests on the bank like a battle ribbon on a general's chest. There's another Judas tree in the next town — a maple again — and it grows behind the house of some people who have a farm stand. By late August the tree has turned. If I had that stand I'd put aside the summer vegetables on the day the tree changed. I'd stock pickles and other canned goods, maple syrup, heaps of pumpkins and winter squash, and the like, and beat the market trading in autumn fare, whatever the calendar said.

Some time in August you can look over a distant hillside through the heavy summer air, and somewhere on it, if it's a big hill, you'll find a single scrap of red, or orange, on the wall of green. It's pretty; any bright color is pretty. But that tree is ominous, too, for it means one thing: an end to ease. The summer is over, that scrap of color says. It's over: I proclaim the fall. Like its namesake, the Judas tree's purpose is betrayal.

AUGUST 1984

Autumn

Woodburners

FIFTEEN years ago, when you couldn't vote in the state of Vermont unless you heated your house with wood, no intelligent adult was without an opinion on what was the best firewood. Oak, beech, hickory, and the rest, each had its legion of proponents: one or another of them burned hotter, burned longer, made less ashes, made more coals. Ash wood, as I recall, was most widely accepted at the time as the philosopher's stone of fuel.

I was never so certain, myself. It seemed to me that the best wood came from the tree that grew closest to the woodshed. In an age of faith where firewood was concerned, I was an agnostic.

Since then, woodburning has fallen off. The debate on oak versus ash seems sometimes to have become as quaint as that over the relative merits of the barouche and the hansom. I still burn my share of wood, however, and I find, now that conviction is irrelevant, that I have entered upon a certainty with respect to firewood — not as to which is the best wood, but as to which is the worst. The worst firewood is butternut.

It doesn't look like lousy wood. The butternut is a substantial, broad-leaved tree with beautiful, pale brown wood having a silky, close grain and a perfectly respectable weight — when fresh cut, that is. Let that wood dry, though, and the same husky chunk of butternut that you heaved onto the stack when it was green now feels like a piece of stage-prop wood made of foam. In a fire it burns like a match and then disappears utterly, leaving a half cup of cold and worthless powder. You might as well try to heat your house by putting a handful of cigarettes into your stove as burn butternut. Fortunately, I have at least a year's supply.

I WAS sitting around out back when my neighbor on the next hill started up his chain saw. It was a good, hard, blue morning — one of the first real fall mornings of that year, with cold shadows and a warm yellow sun. A good morning to get in some work on the woodpile, George probably thought. Better him than me. I was content to listen. I could tell George was cutting small stovewood. His saw idled, idled, then its engine's noise rose in pitch briefly with the cutting stroke, then it idled again. The cuts were short, the idling between cuts long — as George or somebody helping him went to set up the branch for the next cut. He was making sticks for his kitchen range.

To the south another saw started up. The man who has the woods there lives in the village, but he and his boy come up here to cut wood. They were cutting fat logs. Their saw scarcely idled, but ran for long stretches at full throttle, the pitch of the engine noise rising and falling as the sawyer rocked the saw in the cut. Farther away, in the valley, a third chain saw was now to be heard with the others. That one was either an uncommonly big saw or it had a bad muffler, I thought, for its engine sounded deep and loud.

The noises of the saws with their different tempos ran together and combined to produce a kind of symphonic effect. It wasn't sweet harmony, no, but it wasn't unpleasant, either — a far-flung autumnal chorus of machinery. George's little saw sounded to me like A-flat, and the log cutters to the south were about F or F-sharp. Then the valley saw came booming in with the bass. If you could get these fellows together, I thought, you'd have no trouble filling a hall: the Green Mountain Trio, in concert this week (and the next, and the next, and the next . . .)

I THINK I have a weaker memory for winter than for summer. It's a failing that comes home to me forcibly at this time of year, when I learn how remote and unaccustomed winter's usages have become in a few months. I take to spring as though it were a book I've read a dozen times, love, and know nearly by heart, but each year winter is a subject I have to learn again.

Fires. One evening in September the house will at last feel cold. A fire would be nice. At this point I'll be momentarily at a loss. A fire? Ah, now I remember: newspapers, kindling, wood. To the woodshed. There progress is difficult because of the bicycles, wagons, lawn mower, bats, balls, garden hoses, and other warm-season baggage that hasn't yet been stowed away to clear a track to the firewood. The firewood itself, stacked head-high and yards deep, seems unfamiliar, though I've spent much of the summer getting it in. Now the motions I make to take an armload off the top of the oldest stack are hesitant and tentative, at least in contrast with the careless speed the same act will demonstrate in January. I guess I hate to take the first sticks off the pile; hate, having added to the supply since June, to begin the long subtraction. But it *is* cold out here.

Indoors, the interior of the stove is black and cold; last spring's ashes feel damp. The kindling goes in, the paper, more kindling — not in an effective arrangement but any way, for I must relearn the business of fire building. The match, the light. It didn't go. More paper, another match. There it is. From the open door of the stove the firelight shines, winter's light; the heat creeps forth, winter's heat. Here is the season's first fire, a passage one can hardly ignore, and if its building was hardly an Eagle Scout job, what matter? In a week or so I'll be back in the groove. I'll be able to make a fire that will burn.

"O F O R a beaker full of the warm South," the poet cried. It wasn't South Hiram, Maine, he yearned after, or South Kent, Connecticut. The poet was talking about an easy, casual place, a place, in particular, where the snow never ever comes in quantities which are such that you have to outguess it every fall so as not to put things you need in spots that the snow will bury or into which it will be blown or shoved. In a place where snow in significant amounts can cover the ground for half the year, trying to figure out how to accommodate it takes considerable pondering. It's a bit like estate planning, no doubt: you have to take the correct steps now, before your plan actually goes into effect; and therefore you can't wait to see what conditions your plan will in fact have to meet.

For example: outdoor woodpiles. Where do you put them? If you put them near the house, they'll be easy to get at, but if you put them too near, the snow sliding off the roof will engulf them and you'll have to dig the frozen wood out piece by piece. If you put the woodpiles away from the roof-slide zone, you'll have to shovel a path to them when the snow gets deep. If the piles are on the weather side of the house, the snow will bank up on them; if they're in the lee, they may drift up. And in any case you must take into account snow clearing. If the wood is too near your drive or walks, it will be in the way. If it's in the way of a plow, it will be buried or scattered or both. The solution is a woodshed, but it's November. Too late, alas, too late. Maybe next year. For now, stop worrying and do what they do in the warm South: put your wood where your best guess says it will be handy and then go indoors and pop a beaker of the true, the blushful Hippocrene.

W E L L, the wood is in. The shed is full. The long stacks are built, filled, and braced. The ax, the maul, the steel wedges, and the heavy hammer are put away in their corner. The yard is picked up and raked. And inevitably, standing around the woodshed in no order, in silent reproach, are a dozen chunks that could not be made to see the light: the unsplittables.

Unsplittables are crotch-bottom pieces, mostly, or they are pieces where a branch started, or where the wood to be split was twisted, or where it grew in a curve. Not all such pieces are unsplittable, however, and so a refractory chunk is apt to announce itself only in that arresting moment when you strike the billet a mighty blow and your ax or maul bounces off the wood like a tennis ball dropped on a granite step. At that point you may hit a couple of more licks, possibly turning the piece over. You can bring out the sledgehammer and wedges, but beware: unsplittables swallow steel wedges the way quicksand swallows dachshunds — without effect from the point of view of the quicksand and with utter finality from the point of view of the dachshund.

At this point you are best advised to apply to your unsplittables the Way of the East: struggle no more, accept, embrace. That incorrigible block is not a useless unsplittable; it is a yule log, which will light your hearth next Christmas. I myself have a supply of yule logs that will take me through Christmas 2011. You may not need that many, but there are other paths out of the frustrating battlefield where you and the unsplittables vainly contend. Unsplittables make step stools and doorstops. You can paint them white and use them to mark your driveway. You can furtively lose them beside back roads late at night. What you cannot do is split them.

S P L I T T I N G firewood is widely appreciated as exercise for the upper body and as an aid to reflection, but the work deserves to be better known as an adventure in connoisseurship in the most rarefied realm, that of the nose. We have been given our five senses to discriminate, to mark differences and similarities between things. Smell is the finest discriminator of all; learn to use your nose while you're splitting hardwood, and it will open for you a rich volume of distinctions.

Compare the heavy smell of olives which comes from a fresh-split block of red oak with the similar but far more delicate smell of white oak, or with the smoky, almost musky olive smell of butternut. Beech wood is faintly sweet; paper birch has a stronger, sweeter scent; and black birch smells like bubble gum. Maple, to me, has little character besides a kind of vague vegetative smell, and ash is odorless. No doubt a finer nose than mine could make something of the last two woods, as well.

Let no one imagine wood sniffing is a mere frippery. The potential is there for hard financial advantage. Why couldn't a really educated woodpile nose attain the kind of refinement we read the whiskey tasters of Scotland possess? They can sniff a glass of Scotch and tell you not only which district it came from, but which glen, which brook, which distiller. Since there's a good deal of money in Scotch, a lot can hang on the findings of an expert nose. Why couldn't the same apply to wood sniffing? Firewood dealers are a tough lot, almost the last of the old-time freebooting capitalists. The buyer needs all the help he can get. A sniffer who could knock ten bucks off the price of a load for an off-scent would be a valuable man.

Big & Little Animals

ALL through the New England hinterlands you find places called Beartown. It is evidently a name given by the old inhabitants to remote, wild districts that resisted settlement. Beartown was the deepest boonies, the other side of the mountain, where the land was so steep and so broken that even the ruggedest farm couldn't hope to hang on. A place, in short, for bears and not for people.

I know of six Beartowns in my state. In many of them conditions have changed some in the years since they were named. Those vertiginous mountainsides that couldn't be made to grow corn or even hay now yield abundantly the crop Recreation. These days, the bears of Beartown get around on skis and den up for the winter in condominiums that cost more than most bears make in an entire career. Bears who can no longer hack Beartown prices are obliged to move on. Where do they go?

My own community is no Beartown; it's pretty tame. But in the past couple of years, bears have begun turning up over here. My neighbor on her early walk sees them: big bears and little ones, going here, going there. Now, I don't know whether these bears are taking our neighborhood up or down, but that they are changing it I have no doubt. I was raised in a big city, and I understand these things. Pretty soon Beartown will be right here. For my part, I don't mind the prospect at all, but not everybody will feel the same way. And I'm not sure the schools can take it. Bears have little bears. In ten years you'll have a bear on the board of selectmen, bears will own the gas station, the store, and the whole town will have gone to — well, anyway, not to the dogs.

T H E chipmunks have lost their wits — what wits they had. It is ancient wisdom that those whom the gods wish to destroy they first make crazy, and chipmunks at this season are all the proof anyone needs that ancient wisdom is in at least one case correct, for in the fall they go crazy and they pay dearly for it.

Driving along the back roads you will see them. A chipmunk will appear at the side of the road. He will race out onto the road for four or five feet, then he'll stop, turn, and race back. Then, as your car gets nearer and nearer, he'll race out again, then back. He never quite makes it across. In his haste and irresolution he doesn't care about cars. You can see how we lose a lot of chipmunks.

The chipmunk's fall road running is accomplished at great speed and invariably with the tail held straight up like a flagpole. It sounds like a stylish performance, but it isn't; it's a spectacle of desperate indecision. The little thing goes out, goes back, goes out, goes back — all in a panic. What's his hurry? He's not busy gathering nuts for winter. Chipmunks sleep all winter; they don't need a store of nuts. He's not in a mating-season frenzy. Chipmunks mate in the spring and early summer. Is there some recondite effect in his brain produced by decreasing daylight? I doubt it. After all, other rodents don't go in for these fits of scurrying back and forth across the roads.

That's why I think someone has it in for the chipmunk in the fall, someone who drives him to immolate himself in his sudden dashes out onto the roads, someone who, it almost seems, makes him hesitate to cross the road until it's certain he'll be flattened. But who this one could be, and what he has against the chipmunk, are more than I can say.

September 30. On the last afternoon of the month, I walked through the woods to the beaver pond that lies at the head of the brook. The woods were dry underfoot, and the colors of the autumn leaves were a little off, a little dull, as they become at the end of a dry summer.

The beaver pond is, I guess, several acres in surface area. It's been here longer than I have, but it can't be ancient, as there is standing dead timber almost all through it. I don't think it's deep — three or four feet, perhaps. There's a big dam at the southeast corner, maybe fifty feet long. I stood at one end of it and looked out across the pond and listened to the sound of water trickling through the dam. Out in the middle of the pond two beavers swam back and forth. They swam in opposite directions with their heads and a little of their backs above the water. They knew I was there, I'm sure, but they showed no alarm; when I left the dam and went around the pond to a point closer to them, they casually shifted their position so as to keep most of the pond between us. Presently one dived, then the other, and they were gone.

I thought I was lucky to see the beavers by day. Normally they are active only at night. At the end of the season, I suppose, they put in extra hours to bring to the pond a full winter's supply of cut branches, whose inner bark they eat. Up on the bank beside the pond, cut trees were everywhere, many of them quite large and at a considerable distance from the water. The beavers evidently fell the tree, then cut the branches and drag them to the pond. They are big, strong animals, but it must be heavy work. I felt I was keeping them from it and so turned toward home.

Color

THE newspapers, the radio, and the television announcers all proclaim it: the peak of autumn color has arrived in the northern part of the state. *Peak Color.* Consider the thousands of visitors — perhaps more to the point, consider the millions of dollars — that are poised on that peak, waiting to come north, where the leaves are red and yellow. Peak color is no child's play; it's big business. So much is clear. Less clear is its real meaning. Peak color is when the leaves are . . . what, exactly?

The positive, factual announcement of the timing and location of the peak of autumn color, often made as part of the weather forecast, gives a kind of quantitative, scientific character to the idea of Peak Color. You imagine a scientist in a lab coat viewing an autumn hillside through a complex piece of equipment, making arcane calculations, and nodding curtly to his assistant: "That's it, Spencer: Peak." But in fact, peak color isn't the speed of light or the acceleration of gravity. It's when the leaves are . . . well . . . best, nicest, *most beautiful.* Undoubtedly, the peak could, in principle, be reduced to a number — perhaps the ratio of leaves that have turned color and remain on the trees to leaves that either have not turned or have turned and fallen. Who's going to count? Peak Color can only be an empty mathematical fiction. Let it be what it is, a pleasant impressionistic image.

Peak color is like the average taxpayer or the height of the rush hour — a phenomenon more discussed than examined. But if you can't count the peaking leaves, you can count the leaf-loving peekers, and you can count the money they leave behind — to the last quarter and dime. *There* is science, and the peak itself is quickly forgotten.

SEEING is learning, and learning is putting the question to nature. For the past four years, in the first couple of weeks of October, I have kept notes of half a dozen sugar maples in my neighborhood, returning to the same trees year after year. I wanted to see whether the leaves on each of these trees turned the same particular color in different years. I had set myself to examine, in specific terms, the small, individual effects that go to make up the immense spectacle of the autumn leaves in their colors.

Some of the maples I have kept track of are saplings, most are mature trees, and one is a giant of probably two hundred years. Some grow in the woods, some in the open. The four autumns in which I have watched the trees have been various, too: some were dry, some wet; some early, some late; some warm, some cold. My methods have not been rigorous. I have made sure I was comparing the same trees from one year to another, but to judge the colors of the trees' leaves I've relied on notes and memory and not, for example, on photographs.

The colors I have seen on the maples have ranged from a deep russet orange to pale lemon yellow. In general I have found each tree turning the same color year after year. In some cases a tree has turned a darker shade of its characteristic color one year than it has the next; but I have never seen a tree that turned orange one year turn yellow another. It's my impression that the trees are apt to turn darker shades in dry years when leaves have turned a little early — but I haven't kept notes on weather and so can't be sure. From such casual, simple-minded observations no large results will come. But small results, such as the discovery that each maple tree has as a rule its own fall color, were all I aimed to get.

F O R every show that nature puts on spectacularly to an audience of millions, it puts on a hundred little, fleeting exhibitions for one or two who happen to pass by. In this our finest month, the air is like a shot of brandy, the sky is a limitless blue, and the country roads glow like the aisles of a cathedral, for the light comes majestically through the turning leaves of the hardwoods as it does through the stained glass of a great rose window. October is a feast for all the senses; people come from around the world to attend at it, and who can blame them? They drive through the hills, or they simply sit and look out at the spectacle laid before them.

No one is suggesting that we should parse our autumn and try to resolve it into its constituent phenomena — so many days of cool, clean air, so many gold and copper hillsides — but any who are lucky and alert can also enjoy smaller, momentary shows. Leaf fall offers one of them. Every one of those billion, trillion leaves must come down. How will they do it? Most days, the leaves seem to fall slowly, by ones and twos, here and there. You'll notice one out of the corner of your eye, or you'll pick out another and follow it down. It's as though each leaf had its own moment to fall.

Then on other days all the leaves will briefly fall at once, like a flock of birds that turns suddenly in flight, flashing their wings as one. For a moment the air will be crowded, thronged with falling leaves. I understand a single tree will sometimes lose all its leaves at once and in an instant stand bare. You'd expect to see that on a windy day, but often moments of sudden leaf fall come on still days, when the drifts of leaves slip down through the quiet air like bright coins dropped into a pool.

THE automobile, that good and bad machine, might have been invented for dwellers in the hill country in autumn when the leaves are at their height. Whatever its depredations on the landscape in other respects, the auto is the best way for those who live and work among them to see the fall colors. That's because a drive along the lanes and over the hills gives you a view of the countryside that is constantly changing, constantly renewed.

If you live in the northern forestlands, where the fall colors are best, it's easy to overlook them. The roadsides, brooks, and hills are too familiar; you see them every day, every hour. The landscape disappears. Across the valley from my house is the side of a mountain. I've lived with it for twenty years, but I don't suppose I've really looked at it more than a dozen times. To adapt Sherlock Holmes's famous admonition to Dr. Watson, I've seen, but I've failed to *observe*. To observe, you need to have your customary sights and perceptions shaken up, turned around.

That's where your car comes in. You need to get out and around. You needn't go far, just take a spin around your neighborhood, enough to give you some new angles, some different paths. Pace is also important. You need to see the landscape passing before you at a fair clip so the colors take on a kind of cinematic energy. You also need to see the leaves at varying distances: now you're enveloped in colors as though you wandered inside a kaleidoscope; now the colors withdraw to a far hillside. It's from a car that you can best get the shifting, self-renewing sense of the autumn leaves that full enjoyment of them may require if they're your home.

EVERYONE loves the autumn leaves that crowd the hillsides and roadways with their last bright show, but there is another, lesser spectacle of the leaves in fall that doesn't get much press. It is a more moderate display. It's not for everyone, but it has its place in the season for those who know it. To catch it you have to seize the moment.

On the first day the fall color seems to have passed its peak and the trees begin to look bare — that very day — go to the woods. The show is there, where the newly fallen leaves cover the ground and spread their colors out among the trees and undergrowth at your feet. The woods you walk through in these few days seem to have been furnished with a Persian carpet — rich, deep, woven with every red and yellow that nature has. Several Persian carpets, in fact. For every kind of tree there is an autumn color, and a careful observer ought to be able to walk through the woods in these days with his eyes fixed steadfastly between his feet and call off by species all the trees he passes as he treads the maples' scarlet, birches' gold, and ashes' deep purple.

The leaf carpet is fleeting; its riches last for a couple of days, no more. There is a darkness to the colors of the autumn leaves lying on the ground that they don't have when they're aloft. The autumn sunlight has gone out of them; the life has gone out of them. Science will tell you that life went out of the leaves weeks earlier, before they began to turn from green. The leaves in autumn, despite all their color, are dead tissue. For my purposes, however, their life has continued and improved until now, when I can find them lying everywhere in the woods, their colors subdued, their substance beginning its quick, quiet return to earth.

Flowers & Others

"NATURE'S first green is gold," the poet says. So is its last. In the dusty final weeks of summer, when the air begins to feel thinner and the cool of night keeps through to midmorning, the goldenrod arrives upon the meadows and roadsides in the year's last major show of bloom. Maybe goldenrod's being the flower that closes summer's shop is the real reason it bears the ill reputation it does; in fact the plant is innocent of the main charge brought against it.

Goldenrod is blamed for the late-summer sufferings of the hay fever–prone. The profuse, richly yellow flowers indeed *look* as though they must spew out pollen by the ton. But goldenrod's pollen is disseminated by insects and is heavy and sticky. By one estimate only 1 to 2 percent of airborne pollen at the height of the hay fever season comes from goldenrod. The culprit is ragweed, which blooms at the same time as goldenrod and whose wind-borne pollen fills the air. Ragweed's flowers are tiny, however, and so its wickedness goes unnoticed.

Far from being a nuisance, goldenrod *(Solidago)* is an admirable plant and formerly was a valuable one. In the Old World it was believed to heal wounds, and goldenrod was imported into England as a medicinal until somebody found it growing wild in London — at which point its healing power was forgotten, the public being unwilling to accept the virtue of a plant that was no longer rare. The American Indians made a yellow dye from goldenrod, and during the Revolution, real tea being in short supply, our colonists drank a concoction they called Blue Mountain tea, made from the plant. More recently Thomas Edison invented a way to make rubber from goldenrod, but the process was too costly to be commercially feasible.

"For the grapes' sake, if they were all," the poet writes again, "For the grapes' sake along the wall." He is imploring the warm autumn day to linger, to withhold its wind and frost and spare the year from winter one day longer. He addresses himself to the characteristic phenomena of the season: the circling crows, the falling leaves, the mists. But the wild grapes, his final image, are as eloquent as any fruit in nature's garden.

Their vines twist and writhe over the stone walls and through the woods like pythons, heavy and dark, as thick as your arm. They can climb trees, covering smaller ones entirely with their broad leaves and creating gloomy little bowers. They hang stoutly from the bigger trees, like the rigging of a tall ship. Grapes seem to thrive best along the roadsides, though, surging over the weeds there, mounting the coarse shrubs and saplings, hanging their infant clusters of fruit like green pearls, just beyond reach. Their tough leaves are deeply lobed, vigorous. By the end of summer, they're tattered and dusty. They droop beside the road.

The grapes themselves are unpredictable. Some years there will hardly be a bunch, some years their weight will make the vines bow down like willows. In a good year the grapes are fat, the size of marbles, their color a deep inky purple, as rich as sin. And as forbidden, at least in the case of the grapes in my neighborhood, for as delicious as they look, they are ferociously sour. Only a partridge could be fed by them, a partridge or a poet. They make better poetry than they do jam. Best leave the October grapes alone, then, and let them, aided by art, tell the tale of this most feeling month, which cannot end, and must.

Tools & Tasks

WHAT tools do you really need to garden with? Well, gardening is digging; you need a spade. You need something to use on the weeds. You need a knife. Three tools: reduced to its simplest, gardening surely requires little more. Of course, many specialized tools are helpful. They speed and improve a number of gardening jobs. Therefore, various hoes, rakes, forks, shears, and so on become more or less necessary to most, maybe all gardeners. Nevertheless, when you have got your essential three tools and a couple more, you enter a realm in which garden tools take on a curious, exotic, overevolved look, like the frail offspring of a languishing aristocracy.

I'm thinking of one tool in particular that I inherited some years ago. It's for trimming the grass around your flower borders. At least that's what I think it's for. I can't be certain, for the tool in fact does practically nothing. It's a pair of old-fashioned flat-bladed hedge shears set on tiny wheels and attached to a shaft that ends in a trigger-grip like the one on a caulking gun. The whole affair is the size of a golf club. You're evidently meant to roll this contraption around your border, working the grip and clipping away at the grass. But unless your lawn is as smooth as a billiard table, those tiny wheels won't roll over it, and the trigger is a sorry affair that does no more than make the blades of the shears nod to each other in passing. In a real garden, and in terms of its intended function, this object has about as much use as the idiot son of the Graf von Nacht und Nebel. Even it need not go idle on my place, however. I put it in the pea patch to scare the deer.

T H E storm windows on this house are not those intelligent ones that slide conveniently into place each fall and then simply slide back out of the way in the spring, the sashes gliding smoothly along snug metal tracks. No, the storms here are, to put the best face on the matter, *fully detachable.*

There are fourteen of them. They weigh in aggregate a little more than 120 pounds. They are made of wood. They must be toted around, wrestled up, hung in place, and battened down each year, and then in spring they must be taken down and stacked up someplace where they won't get busted and where they will be out of the way. As any child can immediately understand, there is no such place.

Furthermore, my storm windows are something less than tight. They do no harm, but that may be the best that can be said for their weatherproofing abilities.

Fully detachable storm windows have their advantages, however, especially from the point of view of intellectual discipline. Each year you have to figure out which window goes where. A couple of my storm windows have numbered brass tacks on them to give their locations. A perfectly good system, but since no window on the house has any corresponding tack, and no list exists telling what windows numbers refer to, the whole arrangement becomes merely quaint.

For me, assigning storm windows is made possible by the fact that no two of the storms on my house fasten in exactly the same way. Some have big hooks, some have little hooks, some have clamps you screw down, some have wooden latches, some go on with bent nails. You have to match the window with the hardware. It keeps you sharp. You miss that annual mental stretch if your storm windows are any good.

IN the old days householders in my neighborhood would cut evergreen boughs in the late fall and pile them around the foundations of their houses to protect their cellars and floors from the winter wind. The pine, spruce, and hemlock branches blocked the wind until the snow began to fall. Then, when the snow arrived, they held it, affording more protection. "House banking," the pine boughs stacked against the foundation were called.

One or two houses around here still use evergreen branches for banking, but most of us have turned to plastic sheeting. Each year around this time my house, like hundreds of others, gets its feet wrapped like those of a Chinese princess. Some people cover the outer walls of their houses with heavy plastic film clear to the top of the first-floor windows. More often you just run a band of plastic around the foundation from the ground to a couple of feet up the wall and make it fast.

I take a fat roll of plastic and anchor it at a corner of the house with a rock. Then I unroll it along the wall and around the next corner. I staple the top edge of the sheet to the clapboards near the bottom of the wall and nail battens made of sections of wood lath over the staples to secure the plastic to the house. Then I weight the lower edge of the sheet on the ground with boards and rocks. I work quickly. By the time I've gone around the house with my roll of plastic, there are something like 110 feet of sheet hanging out. One year a big north wind came over the field before I had my banking sheet battened down. One end of the sheet was fast, and I held the other. The sheet filled like a spinnaker and pulled me into the air. I was carried by the wind (you can believe this or not) clear to Palm Beach, where I found that few people banked their houses against the winter wind at all and those who did used not plastic, not pine boughs, but hundred-dollar bills.

THE job of setting things about the place to rights for winter holds a telescope up to the spring and summer just past, a telescope that you look through at the wrong end. Events, individuals, mishaps, ideas, plans of May through September appear as if at a great distance through the lens of late-autumn chores. It's an effect that stands the Theory of Relativity on its head: time speeds up, rushes more quickly into the past for the observer who is busy around his home in the fall.

The windowpane that I dislodged in swatting a fly in June, as I fix it in place now, seems to have been knocked loose years ago. When I tear out the frost-killed marigolds, a dank, tough tangle the height of my knee, I remember planting their seeds this spring in the warm, new earth of the garden row; it feels as though that planting happened in another life. I promised I'd mend that fence. Today the project is as remote as the quest for the Northwest Passage. The lawn chairs must be lugged down to the cellar. The company who sat on them in the August heat have returned to distant cities. Now the air feels not far off snow. That visit might have happened to somebody else, in a former age of the world.

Why should this be? In the spring when you're planting, setting out, opening up, you don't see a sharp image of the winter before receding into the past. You're looking forward then, I guess, letting your life expand. In the fall, however, you're moving inward, seeking warmth and light rather than joy. There's a certain pleasure in doing so, a certain security — but there's also a certain regret. Hence, perhaps, the feeling of remoteness of the life just past that comes in preparing your place for winter.

EVERY fall I enjoy watching the war of the leaves waged by conscientious householders in these parts. One in particular I have in mind, the owner of large, immaculate lawns, handsome buildings, and — in the New England way — several stout old maple trees which every year cover his lawns with their fallen leaves to the height of your ankles. The owner waits while the leaves fall. When the last leaf is down, he strikes. Early one morning his lieutenant arrives on the place with a small, wheeled machine driven by a gas engine, which he pushes aimlessly around and around. The machine is apparently a fan. It blows the fallen leaves into windrows. Presently two more fellows drive up in a big truck with high, slatted sides. They rake the leaves from the windrows into bushel baskets, dump the baskets in the truck, and cart the leaves away.

It takes the crew one day. When they're done, the big lawn is an eerie sight. It's in its June condition again: green, smooth, and unmarked by a single fallen leaf. But consider the effort: three men (say twenty-four man-hours), and two machines, the truck and the blower. That spring lawn in autumn is a triumph of leaf disposal organized, manned, and equipped like a military operation.

Contrast leaf disposal around my own place. I have no truck, no blower. I have a wife and a couple of kids with better things to do. I have better things to do, myself. The leaves lie there. The place looks scruffy. I feel bad, but not too bad. And, funny thing: by the time the snow comes, my lawn is nearly as bare of leaves as my neighbor's. How? The autumn wind came along and took care of everything.

Fallen leaves. Rake them if you want, is what I think, but remember what the old poet wrote: "These too the wind shall blow away."

"Science"

NIGHTS in late fall, when the frost is hard and the air clear and sharp, are best for looking at the sky. There is wood smoke on the breeze. Overhead the sky bends over the Earth like the top of a great circus tent, crowded with the familiar beasts: the bull, the ram, the winged horse. About halfway up the eastern sky is a very bright star, and just above it to the right is a fuzzy, vague patch in the sky. That patch, if you have a pair of binoculars, can give you a hint of the excitement of discovery.

The big star below the bright patch is Aldebaran, and the patch itself is the Pleiades. The Pleiades is not a star but a so-called *open cluster* of stars. There are altogether something like fourteen hundred stars in the Pleiades, but only nine are bright enough to have been named. Simple binoculars resolve the cluster into a startling array of hundreds of stars, six of which form a brilliant hook, with the lesser stars scattered among them. The Pleiades fairly leap down at you from the haze of their great distance, and where you saw only a fog you find detail, complexity, and an intimation of the strangeness of the heavens.

Galileo in 1609 pointed his new telescope at the Pleiades one night and found forty formerly invisible stars in one of the early steps in what was perhaps the richest period of scientific discovery in history. In a way, it's a breakthrough that can still be made. Only in the sky can you come close to repeating the discovery of worlds. You can't return to New York Harbor and find it as Verrazano did in 1524, and similarly for the source of the Nile and the Newfoundland capes. The Pleiades endure. They have been found but not changed: the consolations of astronomy.

PLINY the Elder, the Roman scholar whose *Natural History,* in thirty-seven volumes, forms an encyclopedia of the ancient world's knowledge of the natural sciences, education, art, and society, had some quaint ideas about medicine. He believed, for example, that kissing the nostrils of a mule cured hay fever. He believed that an owlet's brains, eaten, were good for a sore throat. Pliny didn't invent these cures; he was a reporter only. Therefore, presumably, afflicted Romans must have been seen every day making unwelcome advances to mules and chasing owlets that ran for their lives. And so the question arises, if Pliny didn't think this stuff up, who did? How did someone get the idea, for a third example, that epilepsy could be treated by feeding the sufferer the afterbirth of a donkey?

Some of Pliny's cures make even other folk remedies look perfectly plausible by comparison. In fact, much of the antique medical lore has a kind of magical logic, rigorous enough in its own way. If you believe the common wildflower Solomon's seal to have some mystic connection with the ancient king of Israel, then it makes a kind of sense to suppose that by grinding up the plant and eating it you will gain fame, wisdom, and the Queen of Sheba for a girlfriend. Beside Pliny's regimens, that advice sounds no more extreme than "Take two aspirin and call me in the morning." Where, in contrast, is the logic behind Pliny's idea that a colicky baby can usefully be served roast lark? We'll never know. One thing is clear, though. Pliny was killed in the eruption of Mount Vesuvius in A.D. 79, when he apparently got a little too close to the action — proving to the most skeptical that a nearby volcano is a sovereign cure for natural history.

EVERYBODY builds woodpiles the same way, and everybody is subject to the same frustration and despair when his woodpile inevitably collapses. But until today nobody has elevated both the construction and the collapse to the level of mathematics.

In making a woodpile you produce a freestanding rectangle that gravity wants to turn into a triangle by causing the upper corners to fall down. To counter this, you buttress the ends of the pile, building towers log cabin–style with pieces of wood placed at right angles to form a square. You build the towers up by the thickness of each piece of wood. Between the end buttresses you stack all the pieces in the same direction. It is this central stack that tends to fall down at the high corners, exerting force against the end buttresses. The higher the buttresses, the more wood they retain, and the greater the forces pulling the whole pile apart. The moment comes when you reach the critical point and an end buttress collapses, dumping the stacked wood inside it.

How can you predict when your woodpile has reached its maximum height, a height at which adding another stick would bring catastrophe? Up to now you have had to guess blindly, but henceforth you can apply the following formula: $h = y - 1$, where h is the height at which the pile will collapse, expressed as a number of pieces of wood of whatever thickness; and y is the height you want your woodpile to be, expressed similarly. Therefore, if you want a twenty-stick-high pile, collapse will occur when you reach nineteen sticks, and so forth. In plain English, our formula states that your woodpile will always fall down just before you quit building it up. And if you needed mathematics to convince you of *that,* you are probably a person of tender years and little experience of our common predicament.

Trees & Men

No part of nature's bounty is better protected against our love than the butternut. In September the nuts — green, sticky, the size of a small hen's egg — are falling. Lying in the grass, they are ankle turners, and because of them the lawn is like a cobblestone street if you have a garden cart or a mower to roll over it. The nuts are no good to eat now. Gather a dozen and spread them on an old window screen to dry. The green outer husk will turn dark brown and be easily sloughed away. Beneath it is the nut.

The butternut is a mighty citadel. Its material must be among the hardest and toughest in vegetable nature. It is ridged lengthwise with raised edges that are sharp enough to cut skin. Within is the nutmeat, its taste like a mild walnut. It's good if you can get it out intact, but that is nearly impossible. Usually you take a hammer to your butternut to crack it. You pound at the nut without result until you overreach and hit it too hard. Then the nut goes off like a grenade, and you are left with fragments of shell and less than enough nut to really taste — and that, mashed. With practice, however, and using a special technique, which I am about to reveal and which comes from the world of music, you can crack a butternut so as to have something to show for it.

Here is how. You need a hard, level surface and a hammer — a full-sized hammer, not a baby. To crack the nut, strike it with the hammer, imagining that you are a xylophonist who is playing the first four notes of Beethoven's Fifth Symphony: you know them — da, da, da, *dum*. The three da's are light taps to let you get the stroke on the nut with your hammer. The *dum* puts it away.

ON the wooded hillsides and along the fencerows, closed down and subdued now against the snow that must be on the way, one tree stands out in this season. It's the white oak *(Quercus alba)*, which, when the other deciduous species have turned bare, remains fully leaved, though all its leaves are long since dead. Other northern oaks — red oak, black oak, chestnut oak — drop their leaves with the other trees. The white oak's hang on, though; they dry to the color of saddle leather. The beech, too, keeps its leaves long after fall is past. The beech is a forest tree, though; it doesn't grow in the open as much as the white oak does, and so we don't see it on a winter hillside.

Through the winter the white oak leaves endure, the tree releasing them a few at a time, as the big blizzards carry the leaves away. Their pale brown is a unique component of the winter spectrum, the snow having covered over the other brown things: dead ferns and brush, the fallen leaves of less tenacious trees. In the middle of the winter when the snow is three feet deep everywhere, you take notice of a brown cluster of oak leaves blowing across an open field like a hare that neglected to turn white.

One day next March or April it will strike you that the white oaks are bare. All their leaves have at last blown away. You'll wonder how long it was since the last one went before you noticed it was gone. When the branches of these oaks are at last empty of leaves, you'll see that the buds of the new year's leaves are full and growing. In a month they will open. It was the Indians, I think, who expected to plant their corn when the leaves of the white oak were the size of a mouse's ear.

NATURE gives bounty and variety, but it seldom gives consistency. Rather, what we can see of nature is full of caprice, trickery, and contradiction — to all of which we respond at least as gratefully as we do to order. No rules without exceptions, no patterns without contraries. No seasons without irregularities.

Consider the witch hazel *(Hamamelis virginiana)*, a common small and skinny tree of the hardwood forest. The witch hazel is blooming right now. Nearly half the year after other plants have bloomed, after the leaves of all other trees have fallen — after the witch hazel's own leaves have fallen — the spidery golden flowers appear on their naked twigs and stand like weak candles in the bare, gray woods.

The witch hazel, then, is stubbornly against nature and, to pagans and other fanciful people, this quality has made it a thing passing strange, a piece of magic. Everybody knows that with this plant's cut branches you can dowse for water. In fact, though, if you can find water with witch hazel, you can do so with any kind of stick, switch, or rod. It's not the stick that finds water; it's you. Nevertheless, witch hazel is the traditional diviner's rod, and that, with the name of the tree itself, attests to its association with whatever is inexplicable, mysterious, dangerous. Witch hazel. The old names for plants are always important, for they were given by people to whom, say, a tree's blooming in the late fall was full of meaning. Whoever called this tree *witch* and believed it was uniquely able to locate water endowed the tree with something like a mind or soul, and did so, I think, chiefly on the basis of finding each year the witch hazel blooming in the autumn woods long after all other vegetation had become still.

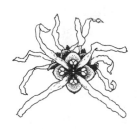

Change

THE multitudes of summer hate to see it end. They keep on coming back. Like an aging tenor or a superannuated generalissimo, a hundred creatures that thrived abundantly in June, then retired with the deep frosts, return on a warm, bright day and take up their careers all over again. But now, although the creatures themselves are real, everything else is different. This is no mere Indian summer, no simple matter of a mild day in autumn: a summer day in November is more like a mysterious moment in a play or movie — it's a flashback, a memory happening now, a dream.

The summer birds have been gone for eight weeks, the garden closed down for six. The trees are bare. A week or two of winter cold has turned the meadows brown and the earth gray. Often there is a thin cover of snow in the morning. The sun is pale and far off. Then two days of flashback supervene, and forgotten life emerges. Little brown snakes curl on the flagstones by the defunct flower garden. Chipmunks are seen poking about. The paper wasps wake up in their cold cracks and buzz around the eaves. Hibernating butterflies, including my favorites, the big tortoiseshells, bask in the sun on the porch floorboards and fly slowly over the clipped dead flower stalks. Little brown and gray moths suddenly appear in the woods and come to lights at night, just as they did in July.

For a couple of days you're in a kind of dream of summer, but as in a real dream, everything that is so convincingly the same is also profoundly changed. It's as though dreams were lighted differently from waking life, and so it is here; summer is back, but it's summer without the colors, summer without green.

NOVEMBER 1993

Care of Gardens

THERE was a freeze last night, or pretty close to it. Cold spots have been near to freezing for several nights. The land has brought forth a peculiar final harvest of old sheets, blankets, bath towels, and bedspreads. Careful gardeners use them to cover their plants and protect them from the frost. Strange fruit: humped and lumpy blankets in their soft colors spread over huddled squashes. As you go about your business in the early morning, you'd think a family of giants had come into the town the night before and, finding no room at the inn, had flopped down to sleep in people's melon patches and cucumber beds. In my own garden we hung sheets over the staked tomatoes, pinning them snugly in place. In the morning it looked as though a medieval army was preparing for battle with its pavilions ranged up the hillside.

This great New England White Sale that gets staged each year at frost time is a little silly in some ways, isn't it? These are vegetables, after all, that we're cosseting, not children, not jewels. Can you bring yourself finally to eat a squash that you've tucked in each night? We might as well go the whole hog and bring the cucumbers into the house. We could clean up the spare room for them and make up the bed, as though they were traveling cousins.

Still, if we are awfully solicitous of our gardens in these parts, our habit of emptying the linen closet on their behalf in the fall does give us a unique way of knowing one another. Down the road is a man who covers his garden with the same sheets and blankets, arranged in the same order from one year to the next: here a blue blanket, then three yellow towels, and so on. That's a real gardener. How does he remember? And who would have guessed that stern, steady Mr. and Mrs. Quackenbush slept on flowered sheets?

OCTOBER 1986

SOMETIME in the month that spans the last half of September and the first half of October, the frost comes. Often the first hard frost seems to pull its punch to begin with, playing cat and mouse with gardens, flower beds, and the more delicate wild vegetation. One night the frost will make a light pass only, as if to flick the garden with its paw, claws sheathed. The next morning only the tips of some of the leaves on the more tender plants will be black with frost's burning. It will look as though the frost just slipped up to the garden, peeped in through the fence, circled, and silently slipped away. This is the kitten frost.

A couple of no-frost nights will follow, with warm days. The leaves that were touched by the kitten frost's playful tap will fall away, and the gardens will appear to perk up. Then one night the first hard, killing frost will come down all at once, devastatingly — the tiger frost. The cat-and-mouse play will be over, and the cat will have won again. In the morning the garden will look like an explosion in a bat colony: blasted, blackened plants, knocked down, lying everywhere. How could a place so vividly full of life as a garden have been reduced overnight to such a ruin? The squash vines will be black, lank, and somehow greasy-looking, their leaves like collapsed umbrellas. The tomatoes will be in a similar condition, and all the fight will have gone out of the cucumbers. You might as well pull them up, cut them off, and drag them away. Take up the stakes and poles, roll up the climbing fences. If you're going to turn over the earth this fall, you'd best get to it. In another couple of weeks the garden will be hard underfoot, the frost having gone into the ground.

I BELIEVE I would plant potatoes in our garden each year even if none of us could eat them, just because I like to dig them up. There can be no harder work than harvesting potatoes in a real field, but over a couple of rows it's pure fun: the vegetable equivalent of fishing.

Only with potatoes does the harvest become a search, even if it is a childish, closely confined search like an Easter egg hunt in which all the eggs have to be hidden somewhere in the parlor. With other underground vegetables, there is a top directly attached. You can walk right up to your carrots or radishes and pull them out of the ground. Potatoes are more remote.

Green Mountains I plant and Kennebecs — big brown baking potatoes with a hide like a rhino's knee. Our thin, acid dirt doesn't grow many good-sized ones, but that only makes the harvest the more exciting. I come into the patch with my garden fork. Down the potato row the plants have died and lie prostrate, yellow. I stick the fork gingerly into the first hill, below the dead plant, and try to use the fork to break up the hill. Pretty soon I'm down on my knees, the fork put aside, feeling among the dirt, stones, and roots. My fingers rake out a couple of marble-sized minnow potatoes, then a larger one the size of a child's fist a bluegill. I feel something else under there, some thing big, but it turns out to be a stone. Under the next hill there's nothing but a few minnows, under the third a good perch, and then, almost seeming to spring out of the earth of its own act, a beauty — a big fat bass of a spud that fills the hand and weighs proudly. The potato patch might not yield another like it, but I am content: it's partly the variety of sizes of potatoes that makes digging them each fall a business full of interest and surprise.

WHY is it that nature so seldom sends the gardener a year that is unarguably either good or bad? The garden's diversity accounts for it: With plants of so many different kinds, it's not in the cards that one pest or disease, one early frost, one dry or rainy month will do in the whole lot of them. On the other hand, it's equally unlikely that in any one year conditions favoring a whole gardenful of various plants will prevail to produce abundance across the board.

Therefore, we have years of cucumber boom and cucumber bust, and similar results for the rest of the crops. In my own case, if I were a better gardener I would take steps to rectify this situation by scientifically giving a hand to whichever vegetables have appeared to fail from year to year. But I'm no better a gardener than I am, and anyway I enjoy seeing what the payoff will be as the garden finishes.

I've noticed that yearly fluctuations in the garden's fortunes are mostly confined to the vegetables of higher estate. It's my impression that the likelihood of a plant's thriving through the vicissitudes of successive garden years is in inverse proportion to its glamour. The lettuces, carrots, radishes, and their humble kind are pretty consistent, while peppers, tomatoes, and squash finish one year in plenty, another in dearth. If I compare my garden to a horse race, tomatoes and potatoes recorded Win and Place last year, while buttercup squash finished out of the money. Almost unnoticed, spinach and parsley ran the course creditably, as they always do. If a figurative horse race may decline into a dog race, therefore, gardening is just like the greyhounds. You know what they say at the dog track: nobody bets on the rabbit, but the rabbit always wins.

I MUST tear out the vegetable garden. It is finished now. I'll till it if I have time and can borrow a machine, but first I must clean out all the old vegetation, wire, strings, and stakes. I'll pick a nice afternoon, one when the sun shines, but it's a cold job anyway. My hands get cold.

The pea wire has to come down. I'll strip the dried vines from the chicken wire, then pull the poles that support the wire. The poles are old. Some of them break off at the ground when I try to pull them up. I'll have to cut some new poles for the peas next year. At the bottoms of their wire cylinders the tomato plants lie dead on the ground like exhausted serpents in a run-down menagerie. I'll uproot the old plants and carry off the cages. I'll yank the bean plants, the peppers, the sunflowers. I'll pull the cucumber vines off their fence and pack the fence away. I see I missed a couple of cucumbers. They're enormous now, the size of footballs and about as good to eat, having gone soft within and their hides having become yellow and leathery. I'll give one of them a kick.

The sun is getting down and the cold is in my feet and fingers, but I'm about done. All the leaves are off the trees. From the top of the garden I can see a white house, one I can't see during the summer, on the side of the mountain to the east. In another month the garden will be under snow. I'm up in the squash patch now, among the ruined leaves and the dead vines that run over the ground, everywhere crossing and tangling. I've never been a neat gardener. There are a number of old squashes lying about still. Now I grab a vine and give it a tug. Twenty feet away, across the confusion of mingled vines, an acorn squash gives a bob, and the vine comes taut where I'm connected to the squash as though it were a pike.

Birds That Pass in the Day

GEESE overhead all day long, day after day, legions of them. Canadas, in their purposeful V formations — though if I think of it, I don't believe I've ever seen geese flying in a true V. The flights I see are ragged oblique lines, or Vs with one leg cut off short. In either case the principle is the same: a slantwise file in which each goose can see where it's going and each goose except the leader can see and be seen by at least one other. The same arrangement allows the stronger, older geese in the front of the line to ease the work of the ones behind by breasting or parting the air for them, just as the leader of a party on snowshoes breaks the trail. So, with their journey well planned and organized, the wild geese pass on to the south, sometimes a mile in the air, and all the time they carry on a constant clamor of honks and yelps that for me is the one most exciting and poignant sound in life.

Isn't it odd, though, that migrating geese should make such a shout? You'd think they'd save their breath for flying. I haven't been able to find in bird books an explanation for the apparently superfluous clamor of geese in migration, but I wonder if it isn't related to that intelligent flight formation of theirs. Geese fly fast, much faster than you might think watching from the ground. And within their flights, as you can see if you look carefully, each goose is constantly changing position, moving ahead, falling behind. Now, except for the last goose in the formation, none can see all the others. Therefore, in order to avoid a pileup, wouldn't they need some means of knowing each other's movements? Maybe that magnificent uproar is nothing more than, for instance, "Okay, George, moving up on your left."

T H E partridge is not a large bird. It's smaller than a crow, not a great deal bigger than a jay. It seems bigger than it is because it makes a big commotion: the partridge is the land mine of the fall woods. With a sudden blast among the dead leaves, it bursts from under your very feet and goes racketing off into the woods, its wings making a noise like a great flail. You get the impression of a sizable bird, when all you really have had is a sizable scare.

There is no wilder bird in the woods. Don't look for the partridge to come up to your window and partake prettily of the store-bought seed you spread for less rugged species that have made their peace with men. The partridge is unreconstructed. It stands by the meager winter woods and eats rough because that's the way a partridge ought to do. The partridge is like the old mountain man years ago who walked ten miles into the village and ten miles back every day along the new road. When someone asked him whether a car wouldn't make the trip easier, he said, "It would." When he was asked why he didn't get one, he said: "We don't have — autos," making it clear that the contempt he allowed himself to express on that occasion was more than worth its purchase by a twenty-mile walk.

The partridge has two selves, one down, one up. In summer it lives in the hardwoods and brush country. It's a retiring bird then, a shy bird. In the winter the partridge moves into the evergreen thickets, and at that time, too, it stays pretty low and slow. In the spring, however, the mother partridges are out with their broods. You see them briskly crossing the dirt roads; you see them along the meadow's edge. And in the fall the partridge plays its trick, popping out of your back pocket and zinging away once more into the gray woods.

N O V E M B E R 1986

MOURNING doves, nearly always in pairs, sit in the middle of the dusty road. If you approach them in your car, they wait until the last second before annihilation to spring up and fly off. More than once I have hit the brakes when a pair of doves vanished beneath the front of my car, but they always get out in time. Daring must run in the dove family. Think of the similar antics of the mourning dove's funky urban cousin, the pigeon, who plays the same desperate game with taxis and buses all over the world.

This dove is one of the beloved birds of heraldry, with the eagle, the owl, the pelican. It is the bird of the gentle feelings: peace, devotion, constancy. Its slender, delicate form, its soft colors, its peaceful life, and its habit of flying and feeding in pairs, provoked the old writers into orgies of sentimental anthropomorphism. Audubon made sure to paint his doves as an epitome of wedded bliss, the female "listening with delight to [her mate's] assurances of devoted affection."

Its call is the dove's most famous trait — a monotone *ohh-oh-oh-ohhh*. To me that song is full of subtlety, playing on our enduring Victorian will to melancholy. Most feel the call is a sad sound, hence the bird's name. The New England ornithologist Forbush referred to it as a "pensive moan." But it's all in when you hear it. On an afternoon in September there are things to be pensive about: the year passes, time and life pass. Maybe there is a certain sadness in the season itself. But who can hear the dove's call in April without welcoming its announcement of the softer months to come? It's the same bird, the same sound. Let it remind us that, wherever else they are, the seasons are in our heart.

SOMETIME in November the chickadees will turn up around the houses and yards again — after the summer birds have departed, cold has killed the summer insects, and all the leaves are down. Their unobtrusive arrival is a last, minor sign of the turning year. The chickadee is the caretaker bird. Like his human counterpart who comes to houses in late fall after summer residents have left and sets things right for winter, the chickadee appears all alone one gray afternoon before snow and sets to work.

The chickadee has a different role and a different set of habits in fall and winter from what he has in the warm months. Like the caretaker, the caretaker bird has to live, so he has another job in summer. Then he is practically unseen, at least by me. He sticks to the thickets and brushy meadow edges and tends to his nest and young. The chickadee is often the small shadow-bird that you can just see hopping about in the tangle, but he's silent and you overlook him for the colorful summer birds that have star billing: the cardinals, orioles, tanagers, redstarts, and the like.

In the fall, though, the caretaker bird is back and can be found poking intelligently around the house one chilly November day. The chickadee won't drain your water pipes, or see to it that the shutters are fastened tight, or the snow fences are put up, or the foundation banking is in place. He won't do any of the things a real caretaker does. He's a caretaker of the spirit. He's here to help see you through the long winter that's ahead. If you give him seed — and sometimes even if you don't — the chickadee will keep you company from the first November day when he shows up, right along through the deepest cold and snow, and on into another spring.

THE geese passing overhead in a great arrow in the sky are first heard and often never seen at all, especially now. Each spring you're expecting them, but in autumn their voices are a surprise. For a moment it's not certain where that noise is coming from; sounds in the sky seem to come from everywhere. And then, geese overhead don't sound like themselves. Half a mile up in the sky they are talking or shouting, but their clamor comes down to us faintly, obscurely. They may sound like a creaking gate, a football game, a radio in the room next door, barking dogs, a brook, a marching band. When you realize it's geese making that far racket, you look up and try to find them in their pointed files flung out against the sky beating south as straight as a line. When you first see them, they seem to go so slowly, but then they are out of sight, and in a minute more they are out of hearing.

The first flight of geese I remember taking special notice of was headed right down the line of Second Avenue in New York one fine fall day twenty years ago. In New York you can't hear geese honking the way you can in the country because the city itself makes too much noise. Nevertheless, there they were, silent but eloquent, for there is something about the sight of geese flying north or south that plays tricks with what we know of time, as though a mirage has descended to beguile history. Geese were flying over Manhattan when that extraordinary island was a rocky woodland bright with squirrels and little birds; and for some reason, when flying geese are in your thoughts, that doesn't seem so long ago. What is it about the seasonal flights of geese that for a moment makes our world seem more temporary than it is?

The Look of the Land

November 26. This afternoon, walked through the woods, across the brook, and up the hill to hit the power line, then followed the power line to a spot where it looked like you'd be able to see the village. It's hard to get a look out from these wooded hills. The trees close in, and when you come to the top of a rise, expecting to see out over the country, you find another hill, another woods, like the first.

The power line clearing is probably a hundred feet broad. It looks like easy going, but it isn't. The ground is covered with dead fern, wild grasses, and tough, low brush, and it's broken ground, full of ledges, holes, and drops. In the woods you'd be able to spot them, but here the brush hides them.

It's mild today, without the damp and chill of a November day. The clouds are November clouds, though: high, gray, and passing. The power line crosses a hidden brook with steep banks. On the south-facing slope above it are places where deer have lain to get the sun. The grass is flattened down, and the dead ferns are broken and scattered. Yesterday hunting season ended. The deer have this remote little corner to themselves again. It must be strange to be a hunter and leave your job and everyday life behind to come out here and wait all day where nobody ever goes.

Up ahead a hawk passes across the clearing on steady, tilting wings, low above the trees. At the top of the hill where it disappeared the woods part a little, and you can see the highway down in the valley, and a house. Farther off is the top of the steeple of the church in the village. What are they, a mile away, two miles? Not more. But up here are only the wind and the gray sky. From the hills it seems that the village is distant by more than miles. Tiny, noiseless, it might be in another world, another time.

NOVEMBER 1988

Winter

The Look of the Land

ACROSS the road, down at the bottom of the hill, a brook runs through the woods. It runs south alongside this property, then turns east and drops down by pools, rapids, and little falls toward the highway and the river valley. That brook has no name. Its length is less than three miles, and this time of year there is no part of it you couldn't step across. Over its course the brook runs through dark woods beneath big old hemlocks growing above it on steep banks and among hardwoods and brush in places where the land levels off.

If you don't mind scrambling here and there and beating the bushes a little, you can follow the brook right down nearly to the village. It's a pretty rough hike: nobody but deer hunters has much business in those woods at any time, and now the deer hunters are gone. In December most years, the brook is full, but it seems sluggish. The water is black, and in some of the narrower passages there is ice along the banks. The trees are bare. On the ground their fallen leaves are a wet, dull cover — part of the earth again, almost. Some years there will have been a little snow, but along the brook the ground remains bare until the heavy snows begin and the water freezes over.

The brook seems to wait for the snow. In the last of the year it is subdued. Any day it will be changed by snow, by ice, by sun. For now it keeps its quiet course among the rocks and pools. The brook awaits the transformation that comes to the hills for all to see, but that only a few will attend in this unvisited sector of the land. Getting down the brook in real winter is too hard for me; but now, for the last time this year, I can come out of the woods beside the brook where it reaches the bottom of the valley and see the water pass silently under the road and away.

IN years when snow comes late, December furnishes a fifth season not part of other years. I have read some writers in New England who call this interval "locking time." It is a distinctive passage, having its own weather, colors, and themes, as much as the commoner, longer seasons have. A bare December's weather is hard cold, its colors gray and green, and its theme is solitude. Every bird, animal, and insect that is going to migrate, hibernate, or die off is gone, and the population of the land is reduced. Even the people have gone, many of them, and it may seem that nobody is left to keep company with except the deer and chickadees.

The leaves are gone. They no longer show their fall colors, even lying on the ground. In the woods the color in this season comes only from the trunks and branches of the hardwood trees, which are every shade of gray, and from the conifers, which are a dark green nothing like the green of spring. I have forgotten the birches, whose trunks are white and lie on the dark hillsides like silver threads on a woolen blanket.

A bare December is a cold season. It has none of the fading heat of autumn. The skies are seldom clear and blue as they are in the real autumn. It's a winter sky, gray and full of changing clouds. The earth is as hard and cold as an iron spike. The back roads are full of dust because the ground is frozen and therefore dry. It's curious to see a cloud of dust following a car in the middle of winter, but this dust isn't like summer dust. This dust is cold. Every so often the sky will fill with snow, but the snow will stop soon and leave the ground bare again. And then one day the snow won't stop.

BEHIND the very tops of the maples that surround the steep meadow across the road, a distant blue mass enters again its winter presence. Mount Monadnock, fifty miles to the east from where I sit. Ten years ago you could see it from here in all seasons, but since then the trees have mostly hidden it in the warm months. Today I can see the mountain's bright summit and a length of one of its northern flanks.

Mount Monadnock is to New England what Mount Olympus was to the ancient Mediterranean: not the highest or the grandest mountain, not the wildest or the most difficult, but still somehow the sovereign mountain. It is medium-sized at 3,166 feet high and stands alone in the middle of a plain in southern New Hampshire like a clipper ship in a parking lot. Virtually all the great New England authors apostrophized Monadnock. Emerson wanted to build a cabin near Concord to get a view of the mountain, and Thoreau hiked to the summit at least four times, not without deploring, on a visit in June 1858, the papers, bottles, and other trash left on the trails by the hordes of unwashed laborers and mechanics who flocked to Monadnock as tourists.

The top of Monadnock is mostly bald. Legend says sheep raisers in the last century burned it bare to kill off the wolves that came down from the height to raid their flocks. I doubt that's the case, but I don't really know. I have never been to Monadnock, have preferred to enjoy it from a distance and as the seasons reveal it, in the spirit of Rudyard Kipling, who watched the peak from a point near my own spot and wrote that the distant mountain "makes us sane and sober and free from little things, if we trust him."

Care of Houses

SO M E time before Christmas, I lose my race against the snow. It started in September; now it's over. It's a race that probably isn't as important as I make it. With few exceptions, the things I say I must get done before the snow comes are not things that, neglected, would threaten our safety, or our health, or even our comfort. Nevertheless, as winter approaches I feel a need to provide against it, even in unimportant ways, to make things safe, even though they are safe enough. And so each year there is a long tale of closing, tightening, nailing down, cleaning, raking, picking up, covering, burning, battening. I set about these jobs calmly, so as to do each of them right, but as the autumn wears on, I'm hurrying to get done before the snow begins, for a good snow will make half my list of jobs impossible and the other half irrelevant.

Always when snow comes I get caught with a few things still to do. The storm windows get on all right, and the foundation gets banked, but there are usually uncaulked cracks, or there's a new lilac that ought to have its own little snow fence and doesn't get it. I now realize that the fall jobs that don't get done are as important as the ones that do. I set my life up each autumn so that there will be these unfinished works at the end; I never make a list of jobs that has a last job.

I also notice that when the snow finally comes to catch me not quite ready, I am content. I'm glad the snow has come. Am I alone in this? I think not. The autumn race to finish an unfinishable list of jobs before the winter comes down is less necessity than symbol. That there must be work left undone at the end and that we welcome the snow when it comes at last are signs that we know we must learn again each winter to submit.

THIS happens half a dozen times each winter, but I am never ready for it. It is snowing hard at bedtime, and I sleep the way you are supposed to sleep on a snowy night when you're in a warm bed in a warm house. Suddenly I am ripped violently from sleep by a rattling, roaring noise that makes the whole house shake as though the devil were racing the Wabash Cannonball through the cellar. The hour is some black recess of the night, and I am sitting bolt upright in bed, my heart racing, my frightened senses questing about me trying to figure out what is going on. Then I hear the final soft rush and thump from outdoors. The roof. The snow has slid off the roof. I am lying down again.

My roof is metal and steep. It sheds snow pretty easily, and sliding snow plays on it as though the roof were an instrument. There is the delicate swish that a couple of inches of light snow makes as it slips away. There is the louder bumping rush of heavy, icy snow. And there is the full-scale avalanche that shakes the timbers of the house. This is not the best house I have lived in for snowslide effects, though. For the loudest, longest, most unnerving releases of the greatest quantities of snow, you want a slate roof. Slate roofs hold on to their snow, and when it slides it's a big event. I once lived in a big old place that had a roof area a little smaller than a football field. It was all in slate. It held the snow and ice, releasing its burden only a few times each winter. When the snow left that roof it usually took several slates with it, and it came down like a vengeful dragon in a long, grating, crashing roar full of screeches made by the loose slates scraping and skidding along the roof. In that house you stayed awake for a while after the roof let go.

I FIND the coldest nights make me uneasy. When I wake in the morning my senses know before I leave the bed that when I look at the thermometer I'll see twenty below, twenty-five below. The air is perfectly still. Outside the light is weak. When you go out the cold astonishes you for a moment, makes you catch your breath. It takes you by the throat and seems to sear your lungs. In a minute, if you look around, you'll find yourself in a kind of dream world, the peculiar world of twenty below. It's quiet: birds don't call, and no wind rattles the trees.

The world of twenty below is a little like the world underwater. In it, everything takes longer than it should. Common materials are changed in the deep cold: wood, leather, rubber, metals yield slowly, move together with difficulty. Nothing slips along as it should. Machinery, objects, bodies are in a trance of cold. The gears of the car move stiffly; it rolls slowly, if it rolls at all. At night you can go outside and see the stars glitter with a new fierceness in the cold air. In a minute you will feel your ears freezing.

I imagine the deepest cold as a great bell that is slowly, silently lowered over our house by night, sealing it off, isolating it, while we sleep. Our houses were built to withstand visitations of the world of twenty below, but not to thrive on them. Mine is old and drafty. On the coldest nights I lie awake imagining the bell descending, imagining I hear the water freezing in the pipes and the frost ferns growing on the night windowpanes. In the attic a drop of frost covers the point of each roofing nail where it comes through the sheathing. By flashlight, the dark attic is a planetarium.

FEBRUARY is the month of power failures. The snow flies, the wind blows, something gives. The lights go out, go on, go out, go on, go out — stay out. Immediately a vast silence descends upon the house. How noisy the place normally is, you realize, how full of sound the condition you ordinarily accept as quiet: refrigerator, furnace, even lights all contribute to a subliminal domestic hum that has now stopped and plunged you into a preindustrial stillness that is exactly as charming as it is brief. A power failure is like a walk in the rain or a performance by a coloratura soprano: for a little while it's fun, but before too long it becomes a bore and at length an ordeal.

If your power failure occurs at night, as fully three-quarters of them seem to, your first need is for light. Here we have a couple of drawers in which we keep candles that are used for nothing else. They're a motley assortment: votive candles, sloppy red Christmas candles, scented candles, candles in the shape of vegetables, of rabbits, busted candles from other occasions. A dozen of them assembled on the kitchen table enable you, with effort, to read a newspaper.

Having provided yourself with light, you are apt to feel some complacency — until you discover that you have no running water. Even then, you may reflect, the very snow that caused the problem will solve it. What is snow, after all, you ask, but water? Well, it's a case of "Yes, but . . ." In a power failure early in my own career, I smugly put on the wood stove a bushel basket's worth of snow to melt, to find later (much later) at the bottom of the pot about half a cup of liquid. Snow, you will find, converts to water at a ratio that does not favor the powerless.

Roads

IN my state the big trucks that plow snow on the state highways are painted orange. They are dump trucks, ten-wheelers with great curved snowplows that rise nearly to the height of a second-story window. The highway trucks are built to move snow and to carry road sand behind — they aren't built for speed. On a long hill, when you come up behind one of them in a place where you can't go around, you will learn the meaning of delay. You will drain the cup of frustration to the lees. Those trucks have thirty-seven low gears, and to get up even a moderate grade they require every one of them. On a steep hill it would in fact take less time for the driver to park at the bottom and wait for the forces of geologic change to erode the mountain down into the valley than it would for him to drive his truck to the top. Or so it seems to the occupants of the heated line of unlucky autos that accumulates behind the highway truck as it labors on its way.

But now contrast the emotions called up by the same slow-moving truck on a scary night in winter. There are six or seven inches of snow on the road, the radio says, but you can't tell for sure because you can't see the road. The air is a black, blinding whirl of snow. You grip the wheel. You skid. You grip tighter. Then you see ahead the yellow running lights of a highway truck. You greet them as though they were the lights of a warm and friendly inn. You feel the road under your car again and see the plume of snow the plow flings off to the right as it clears the way. Gratefully you join the line of cars that shelter behind the plow and follow humbly in its path. You're all right now. You can follow the snowplow home. The big orange truck, like a good shepherd, will lead its thankful flock slowly, surely, through the storm.

Wood & Fire

LIKE Moloch, the fiery devourer, a minor god presides in my household, demanding burnt sacrifice. This god, however, is not an Old Testament bad guy, but an obsolete construction of cast iron manufactured around 1920 in Taunton, a small city between Boston and Fall River.

In Taunton the Weir Foundry began making Glenwood parlor stoves and ranges in 1879. One of their medium-sized kitchen ranges is a dominant figure in my life each year from September to May. It's black with faded chrome-plated railings, about the size of a lowboy chest, weighs a couple of hundred pounds, and burns wood. It has an oven, six lids on the stovetop, and a threefold system of dampers and draft controls that takes some learning. We use it for heat. When it's fired up and running straight out, the Glenwood can heat the whole house (as long as the weather isn't too cold and you wear lots of clothes and keep moving briskly about).

The Glenwood is a nice thing to have around. In operation it makes comforting sounds — ticks, clunks, wheezes, sighs — and its smell of hot iron can keep you almost as warm as the heat it produces. In looks it's utilitarian. A lot of those old stoves look like iron wedding cakes, encrusted with curlicues, swags, and fictitious foliage. My range's ornamentation is pretty restrained by comparison.

Keeping it fed is a lot of work. On a bitter day, I bet, this range can go through seventy-five pounds of hardwood sticks. In the seventy winters of its existence, that's a prodigious quantity. I imagine whole forests as whirling in a great vortex, being drawn down farther and farther to the last, deepest bottom — in my own kitchen — where in an unending procession the children of Canaan pass through the fire.

AT this house the woodpile is twenty-five steps from the kitchen — hardly a great distance when I have thought to provide the house with firewood by daylight and in good weather. In those conditions, the trip from the house to the woodpile almost disappears: it can be accomplished between thoughts. It is otherwise, however, when the twenty-five steps to the woodpile are in the dark, through ankle-high drifts, and into a driving snow from the north. Then I find walking to the woodpile gives me ample time to imagine, and even to plan in some detail, elaborate structures. It's not so much that time slows down when I must flounder out through a winter blow on an ear-freezing night, but that thought speeds up — so fertile are the minds of the lazy and impractical.

In a matter of seconds I build mental woodsheds, or wood mansions, depending on how arduous the trip to the woodpile is. If I must walk out there through a light rain, say, and load soaking wood to carry back, I can erect a simple pole shed. Six posts, plates, rafters, and some kind of roof — enough to keep the rain off. Half a foot of snow and a good sharp wind, and I can put walls on that shed and endow it with a floor to keep the stacks off the ground. Maybe close up the weather side. Still nothing grand, you see. But now give me a full-fledged winter storm, with a big blow from the north driving the snow in waves, and all the paths drifted over, and I can rear out there to house my wood in a Chartres, a Notre-Dame de Paris. I see gloomy aisles and dark side chapels, vaults and arches, and stained glass soaring above the hushed and lofty nave. And I see the causeway. Yes, a covered causeway, like those tubes that pass from an airliner to the passenger terminal, this one exactly twenty-five steps in length.

Weather Foretold

T H E first big snowstorm of the winter, when it comes, will be announced by signs astronomical, meteorological, and animal — all unreliable — and by signs human, which are a better guide. Halos around the moon, turning winds, and the activities of small birds and animals are thought to predict storm, but they do so only equivocally and subject to interpretation. Some say the sparrows run about before a storm; some say they quiet down. We can't go on intelligence as unruly as this. We need more certain predictors of storm. Let us put the stars and the birds aside and look to our own kind.

Last December I drove halfway down Vermont one day as a storm that turned out to be a foot-and-a-halfer came in from the southeast. The snow hadn't started yet, but there were plenty of signs that it would before long. Among them, no doubt, were birds in particular and significant patterns of rest or activity. I didn't notice the birds. I did notice a man on a bucket loader busily filling a dump truck with sand from a new three-story-high pile beside a town garage. In the villages I passed, people had moved their cars off the street and parked them in narrow driveways or even on front lawns. I saw a couple of people wrestling snowplows out of the weeds and horsing them up onto the fronts of pickup trucks.

I can read these signs. I might ignore a low-flying chickadee, but I won't ignore the portent of the aforementioned driver of the bucket loader and his work, probably because I know what's on the driver's mind. He's got a job ahead of him; he's a little afraid of the storm that's looming, as am I. I can't believe chickadees worry about the weather that they are alleged to foreshadow.

WE know too much about the weather. Its reporting has been influenced by what E. B. White called "the stepping up of the news," the mistaken notion that everything is important. We ought to remember that weather is news, especially winter weather, and that news makes many people rich, but only if many other people want to hear it. Now, real weather is pretty dull, pretty uneventful. In February it snows; it shines; it's cold; it thaws. Nothing new, you see? But weather mustn't be dull or it isn't news, and since commerce must have news, weather is reported on in a way that makes it seem more important, more exciting, and indeed more dangerous than it is.

It comes to this: weather is reported on as if it were war. Consider those ominous "winter storm warnings" and "travelers' advisories" (note the peculiarly modern menace in that bland word — *advisories,* indeed!). The language is that of a people at war, a frightened people whose guardians are those well-turned-out men and women who each night take us over the weather maps. And consider weather maps themselves for a minute. Their mode is military, isn't it? A weather map is an elaborate, violent composition of heavy black bars, blobs, lines, arrows, and figures which resembles the German General Staff's plan for the invasion of France in 1914. The maps make weather seem full of action, will, threat. They make it news.

Hold it. A snowstorm is not a war. It's not an earthquake. It's not a revolution. It's a snowstorm. Maybe we ought to go back to dull weather reports and see if we don't all feel a little better. An old-timer around here was asked, "How many inches is it supposed to snow?" He looked up at the stormy sky for a second and then replied, "It don't say."

IT don't say. But we do. We say a lot. We hear a lot. Too much, maybe. If the weathermen can't scare us to death, maybe they can drown us in erudition. Broadcast weather bulletins inundate us with information and half-understood principles. The forecasters tell us much more than we want or need to know, to the point that, with the weather as with politics, art, and the conduct of life, we are overcome with information and lose our way.

Consider a typical weather report on my radio. A *meteorologist* (note that he or she is not weatherman or an announcer, but a *scientist*), clears his throat and carries on something like this: "A preponderant Arctic system originating east of Great Slave Lake is rapidly autorelocating southwesterly across the Laurentian Highlands, encountering a subsidiary low-pressure configuration emanating from the region of the Bay of Campeche, rendering it probable that should these two meteorological entities converge at high altitude over Churubusco the likelihood of solid or semisolid precipitation will be in the range of 22.1 to 37.4 percent; *whereas* should the Arctic superbarometric eventuality and the Oaxacan subbarometric abstraction fail to effect conjunction before reaching the latitude of the Fishkill Salient, the probability of such precipitation achieves the inverse of the range hypothecated. We'll keep you posted. Now back to you, Edgar."

No, it's not really that bad. But you get the point: a blizzard of data driven by a hurricane of lingo, most of it relevant to places far distant. That's not what we need. What we need is this: "It's going to snow tonight, probably. Probably start about dark. Might snow a foot or so. If you have to go to town, go now. Back to you, Edgar."

E A C H of us, however wedded he is to the skeptical, the empirical, the strictly scientific, has a piece of unscientific weather lore in which he believes implicitly, and this is mine: the smaller the flakes, the bigger the snow. Other signs — what quarter the wind is from, how the air feels, what the clouds are doing, what the winter birds are doing — I leave to those who need them. For me flake size is the one rule.

Time and time again the principle has stood by me. The sky can be leaden and the air dense with enormous snowflakes falling so thickly that you can hardly see across the road. I serenely set out to drive over the mountain on a trivial errand. The Boston stations can be in a panic, predicting a very Judgment Day of a storm, and the clouds can be gathering even as the announcers bleat away. If the first flakes I see are the size of small butterflies, I will confirm my dinner engagement in the next county.

But let the sun still be shining somewhere in the west, and let the radio be placidly announcing the winner of this week's hundred-million-dollar lottery — if snow begins to fall in tiny points that drive before the wind and sting my face a little, if the flakes bounce off the house like thrown grains of sand, then I head for the hatches. I put the car where it won't get buried. I shout to the kids to get their skis, their poles, their sleds, their dog, their cat inside. If the radio were that moment to reveal that I myself had won the lottery and was expected at headquarters to claim my hundred million, I would not venture it. I know that those hard little gnats of snowflakes mean big weather. I don't know why it should be that little flakes go with big storms. I have seen that they do. Small flakes, big snow, is for me the rabbit's foot in the skeptic's pocket. I believe.

THOSE people who believe themselves superior to talking about the weather, and who despise country folk because they are supposed to have no other conversation, miss a whole realm of language and its particular delights. Do not imagine that when we exchange remarks on the weather, we are stupidly, irrelevantly reciting information that we already have. Weather talk is not reporting or description. It's more like poetry or song, and its end is not conveying fact, but the pleasure taken in using our language in a dramatic, even poetic way.

We personify the weather, as a poet would. We give it purpose, feelings, mind. On a day of changing snow, cloud, and sun, we say, "It can't make up its mind what it wants to do." To describe the weather we use poetic figures right out of the rhetoric texts, as when we call a heavy rain a "cow drowner" or a "lamb killer" or refer to the winter wind of this time of year as the "Montreal Express." All weather talk is essentially metaphorical. Its meaning is not in the definitions of its words but in their images and associations: "It's raining cats and dogs."

The best weather talk often proceeds like a play. There are parts: the one who wonders, the one who knows. We ask: "Is it going to stop snowing?" He answers: "It always has." The same dialogue took place last winter, will take place again next. Repetition is of the essence of talk about the weather. We aren't telling each other something new; we're telling each other something old. That's why we engage in weather talk. We could use numbers or any other empty code merely to report on the weather. To enjoy the old, familiar conceits and similes of real weather talk, you need language. Animals and birds, perhaps, and city people too wised-up for weather talk, undoubtedly, can pass on information on the weather as well as we can, but they can't have so much fun doing it.

As a democratic people, Americans are supposed to be mostly indifferent to manners and likewise to all other considerations of what used to be called "good breeding." If that's true, we miss a lot of fun, not because manners are really important, but because to ignore them is to lack a whole system for describing the world and making distinctions between things — and that not only in matters of etiquette, but even in the field of weather.

Consider snowstorms. Clearly, our vocabulary for describing them is pretty poor. There are nor'easters and Canadians, dusters and ten-inchers. Plain fare, at best. If we introduce the idea of *snowstorm etiquette,* we immediately acquire far richer, more informative categories.

As with the etiquette of behavior — that is, real manners — so good breeding in winter storms is almost less a matter of what is said and done than it is a matter of timing, setting, inflection, style. A well-bred storm occurs at night — a weeknight, please, not a Friday or a Saturday night. A well-bred snowstorm knows what it is: a *snow*storm. Therefore it eschews ice, sleet, and rain. A well-mannered storm does not knock out the electric power, any more than a gentleman gets drunk and hurls the hors d'oeuvres against the drawing room wall. A well-mannered storm knows what is enough; it does not make the loutish error of supposing that if six inches of snow are good, eighteen are three times better. Above all, a well-bred storm, like a well-bred gentleman or lady, knows when to take its leave. It does not linger awkwardly an instant over the time it is wanted. It slips fastidiously away in plenty of time for shoveling, plowing, and road clearing to take place. In weather as in human relations, manners are a way of making life easy, sensible, and, especially, predictable. Boreas, take heed.

I BEGAN to suspect that last winter would be something out of the ordinary when I got a Christmas card from the chief executive officer of the Mobil Oil Corporation, a gentleman I didn't remember ever having met. "Greetings, and *thanks in advance for your business!*" the card said. Do I know you? I asked myself.

Six months later — six months and about a million gallons of Mobil's best No. 2 — and I'm in no doubt. By now the CEO and I are — not friends, perhaps, but no longer strangers. You could say we're partners, I guess. Judging by the last statement of my account, it's a partnership that will last for some time to come.

Yes, 1993–94 was quite a winter. In this part of the country it broke a lot of records, particularly for cold, records some of us wouldn't have minded seeing remain intact. As I look back on the winter, it seems to me that the temperature went down below zero Fahrenheit sometime last August and stayed there well into the following May, dipping frequently to points I hadn't realized could be attained on our planet. I had always thought the negative numbers around the seven to eight o'clock position on my outdoor thermometer were there for show. Turns out they're not.

It was a real, old-fashioned winter, everybody said — an interesting idea. The long, hard winters of yesteryear, like its wise and honest statesmen, gallant soldiers, and matchless athletes, are a sentimental falsehood, aren't they? A trick of memory? A trick not even of memory but of shared historical fantasy? Well, maybe they aren't. Maybe the winter of 1993–94 came among us to prove that the good old days were exactly as advertised, and to make us wish them right back where they came from, in the distant past — and to stay, this time, please.

IT'S a funny thing, though, about those same episodes of the deepest cold: as painful as they are, we seem to take a certain pride in them. The first thing on any morning when the forecast has been for extremely low temperatures, I hurry downstairs to the kitchen and look eagerly out at the thermometer. If I see −20, −25, I find I'm pleased, I'm elated, I'm somehow affirmed.

The deepest cold, then, has a kind of kick to it; it becomes an achievement. We hate such bitter cold, we even fear it, but we also find it exciting; we want it to surpass itself. In effect, we're rooting for the cold. The most arctic nights are like the engagements of a local ball team: a source of frustration and affection oddly mixed. Nor are we above a certain quiet bragging on the depths to which our own thermometers sink. Every workplace, on the morning after a big freeze, becomes an arena of fierce competition as the data come in. I once worked in an office where the winter temperature derby was invariably swept by a woman who lived on the side of Stratton Mountain and showed up every morning with −30, −35. We finally had to make her spot the rest of us seven degrees — amounting to a handicap, as in golf.

For the battle of sinking thermometers I happen to be poorly equipped. I live on the east side of a hill in a house that faces east by south. It's a relatively warm spot, a fact for which I'm grateful. Sure, I'm grateful. Except on the coldest mornings when I know my −19 will not hold up for long when the reports begin to arrive from my proud neighbors who live in the cold hollow at the bottom of the hill.

Buzz, Buzz, Buzz

ON the coldest day of winter I'll light a fire in the stove in this room, and presently, when the heat from the stove has had time to soften the cold, there will come a slow, intermittent buzzing from somewhere in the room, as though a patient salesman were ringing the doorbell. Then a housefly the size of a Piper Cub will appear at the window inside, buzzing weakly, climbing up the pane, falling back down onto the sill, buzzing, buzzing.

All winter long the cracks of the house yield up an endless train of fat, lazy flies that issue forth to gather at the windows whenever the room they're living in gets warm enough. Long after most of the fly class of 1984 have succumbed to winter outdoors, these individuals survive past their natural date inside the house. In the way they gather at the windows to look out at the inhospitable winter, they remind me of elderly, well-stuffed gentlemen, members of a venerable and aristocratic club, who from the windows of the drawing room look out at the street, and seeing the changed world out there, are grateful to be old. I expect any minute one of these flies will abruptly rustle the pages of his *Times* and ring for a brandy.

It's not all easy street for the flies that move indoors in the winter. They are still flies, and I squash them when they bother me. The cats in the house love to chase them, especially the kittens, who are electrified by the noisy, struggling flies and try to climb right up the window after them. By springtime the number of indoor flies has been cut down. But there are always a few left around, and it's one of the year's little ceremonies to open the window for the first time in six or seven months and watch those aged flies at last buzz heavily away.

JANUARY 1985

Attention: Snow

ONE day this month you will wake in the morning a little earlier than you usually do, and you'll realize before you're fully alert that something has changed. You can't name it, but there is something that has awakened you. Then a car will go by outside, or you'll look up at the window, and you will understand. Snow. The first big snow has fallen in the night. Last night you went to bed in fall, and now this morning it is winter. You slept in one time and woke in another, like Rip Van Winkle.

Before you get up, lie in bed for a minute and see what it was that advised your sleeping senses of the first snowfall. Quiet advised them. The air, the trees, the house are hushed in the snow. The quiet following snow is different from the quiet in other seasons. What noises there are, are muffled. Light is changed, too. The early daylight when it comes in the window is nothing like the light that came in yesterday, before the snow. It's brighter, barer, for coming in from a white world. If you are up early enough to see the dawn you will see that the sunrise seems much more distant after snow than when it comes over a many-colored horizon.

Some part of you was aware of these changes before you woke. To changes in the weather, in the seasons, we are sensitive, despite our civilized removal from their influence. We never sleep. We are animals yet, a little bit. Politics, money, society, war — their changes can keep us from sleeping, but they can't wake us up. Changes in the atmosphere, in the heavens, in the year, can. The first snowfall you won't hear, or, often, see, but its advent will bring you from the deepest sleep.

LAST night about bedtime a big storm blew in, and now at midmorning the snow has increased; the world is confused, suspended in a gray twilight swirl of wind and snow, silent and, it can almost seem, released from time.

Out my front windows the road has nearly disappeared. An hour ago somebody went by in a pickup; his tracks have about filled in, and no one has passed since. Normally there are people driving up and down the road all day — not in a stream (it's still a country road), but one, then another, from early morning to past dinnertime. Not today. For as long as the storm lasts, the road returns to a quiet farmers' lane where every passing vehicle must be noticed.

The storm has overcome time. Recent history in these parts has been crowded with the new: new houses, new roads, new rules, new things to do, new costs — above all, behind all, new people. People around here have been more and more hooked up, moved together, put in the same boat, whether they liked it or not. For a few hours the storm has undone all that. It has canceled history. It has emptied the roads, it has hidden the neighbors, it has made their houses vanish. The storm has given us the country back. It has restored the state of isolation, or the *feeling*, the conviction of isolation, that was sovereign in country places in the past and formed the unhappy side of the coin of rural independence and personal liberty. Government, science, invention, commerce have moved to banish that isolation, and around here they have pretty much done the job. But in a winter storm, for a time, when the familiar is hidden and the snow closes around, you can feel the old solitude again, for a while. You can savor what was — and at no risk, for the storm will end.

December 20. A big storm is coming. The forecasters are falling over one another to see who can hit the alarm bell hardest. It's early in the winter for a real snow, but indeed, outdoors it looks as though the weathermen might be right this time. The morning was palely sunny, but after lunch a gray iron sky supervened with a keen little wind out of the north. Time to get ready.

Preparing for a major storm is like preparing for war: you take thought not for what you suspect your enemy *may* do, but for what you know he *can* do. First thing, I back both cars down to the bottom of the driveway and leave them facing the road. That way the snowplow can get up the drive and I'll be able to get out after the storm without backing downhill through deep snow, a maneuver that often does not end well. Then I bring a couple of cartloads of fuel in from the woodshed. While I'm outside, I make sure the snow shovel is gassed, oiled, and has a new plug.

Inside I fill the bathtub. Should the storm knock out the electricity, we'll have plenty of water for washing and for operating certain articles of household plumbing, the importance of which is demonstrated with real force by a three-day outage. I check the flashlights to make certain all batteries are either weak or dead. They are. I ask, as I do each year, why we don't have a kerosene lamp. I still don't know. I try to think where the candles are. I fail.

It's nearly dark and the snow has begun. The bare patches and the steps have turned a fuzzy gray. It's supposed to snow all night. Before I quit, I always fill the bird feeder — my last gesture of readiness, the final perfecting touch that sets the whole place safely straight and lets me enjoy the coming storm.

WHEN it is snowing hard at bedtime, sleep is sound and waking is full of anticipation, like the anticipation felt by a child on Christmas morning when he wakes and keeps his bed a minute before getting up, knowing he will find the world excitingly changed by the lights, the tree, the decorations, the gifts. Here, it is the gift of snow people wake to discover, and if the storm has been a big one, it's an exciting moment when you first look out the window to see what the snow has done.

Even if the snow is bad news for you because you must make your way through it to go about your business, there is a quick pleasure in first looking upon its work the morning after a storm. Every dwelling has its own set of impromptu snow gauges that tell you immediately, and more eloquently than a bare account of inches of depth ever could, what size storm has passed. Can you see the stone walls? How deeply is the car snowed in? To the wheel tops? To the door handles? How much of the rhododendron still shows? Where is the woodpile?

At my house the best snow gauge last year was a large metal lawn chair that was left outside. Nobody ever got around to putting it away in the shed with the rest of the summer things. The winter was the snowiest in some years. One morning the chair was up to its seat in snow; another morning the snow was up to its arms. Then there came a hard storm that blew all through the night, and the next day, under clearing, shifting cloud and sun, the chair was gone. I looked for it and saw only the featureless plain of white. For just a second I asked myself what uncharacteristically order-obsessed member of my family had gone out into that blizzard the night before and moved the chair, at last, into the shed where it belonged.

Birds Near at Hand

CARDINALS and redpolls, purple finches and crossbills, the bright birds that bring quick color to our senses in winter, make themselves pretty scarce around my house. I put out seed for the birds, always have, but for the most part I attract winter birds that have winter's colors: chickadees, nuthatches, titmice. The other day I saw a purple finch outside the window. The bird looked like a frozen strawberry, and it lifted my spirits, but it soon went away and I don't insist on its return. The gray birds and the brown birds return. I'm used to them. I think I appreciate them. Let the colorful go down the road.

If you have no fancy birds with fancy colors to watch during the winter, you may be led to look longer at the more mundane birds you do have. That is good luck for you, because the real fun in observing any animal is not in admiring its looks, but in trying to figure out what its life is like and how its mind works. When your store of birds is a few common species, you come sooner to looking at what individuals are doing than you would if your birds were a changing parade of flashy exotica.

Look for actions, look for plans. Chickadees pick up their seeds, but they don't eat them then and there. They fly the seed up to a nearby branch and dispose of it in private, it seems. Why? Nuthatches do the same, I think, but grosbeaks and sparrows eat on the spot, the former with a great smacking of their chops. Again, how do birds take off? Nuthatches and jays seem to make a little leap to launch themselves into flight, but chickadees just start their wings and fly off, I think. I keep saying "I think" and "it seems." It isn't always clear how birds do things. They're quick, and they're nothing like us. It's not easy, looking at birds.

THIRTY or forty yards from my house, at the edge of a meadow, I keep a kitchen garbage dump that I call a compost pile. Four bluejays who live on the property call it a free lunch and avail themselves of its provender liberally in all seasons, but especially so in winter. They rise from the pile with a great flap and squawk as I approach with a new pail of table scraps. When I return to the house, they descend immediately and commence flinging the stuff all over the snow, keeping up a loud palaver the whole time, like a hall full of drunken undergraduates.

Bluejays are the most human of birds. We recognize them easily as creatures that are more like us than most other birds are. What is it we recognize? It's sin. The qualities we think birds have that make them resemble us are never good qualities. The cock is proud, the crow thieving, the goose a bully. Whoever felt kinship with any bird for its charity, devotion, or high-mindedness? The principle extends to animals, but not perfectly. Domestic animals we say may have human traits that are admirable: dogs are loyal and loving, cats dignified, horses stalwart. Wild animals, however, when we find them to have human qualities, have qualities we hesitate to praise: the fox's low cunning, the weasel's blood lust, the bear's clownishness.

Still, we admire them; we admire them all. Bluejays are rapacious, greedy, disorderly, noisy, evidently irresponsible. They are also beautiful; but that bright outfit and rakish crest could not belong to a good citizen. Birds and animals do for us what certain characters in fiction do. The qualities we admire in creatures, like those we admire in some people in novels, are ones we are not so apt to admire in our friends and neighbors.

Tools & Tasks

IF you shovel snow, remember two rules: (1.) the snow is bigger than you are; don't try to move it all at once, and don't try to move it too far; and (2.) the solace of work that is essentially vain, futile, or meaningless is Style — and if you're shoveling snow, then your work is futile, if any work is.

Watch your neighbors, see how they shovel snow. The man you see struggling to pitch an enormous shovel, on which is poised a block of snow the size of a hay bale, is an amateur. If you're his friend, advise him to take it easy, or to get a snow blower. If you're his life insurance agent, insist. In your own snow shoveling, use a big shovel, by all means, but take small bites. Don't heave the snow out of your path if you can help it; rather, just twist your wrist and let the snow slide off the shovel beside the path. And try to get to your shoveling soon after the snow has stopped falling. The longer you wait, the more time the snow has to settle, increasing its density and increasing your work.

Try to shovel with style. Reflect that the goal of snow shoveling is an unsatisfactory one: you will never see the end of it; there will be more snow tomorrow. Still, today's snow must be shoveled. Make the act of shoveling, not the result, the object of your care. Take pains to shovel your paths straight, to make them of uniform breadth, and to cut your corners neat. Take your time. Make unneeded paths, detours, shortcuts, oxbows, dead ends. If you have animals or small children, they will thank you. And you will have the satisfaction of knowing that you have overcome winter in the only way you ever can — by submitting to it, but gracefully and with style.

N O W, as the season of storms approaches, a bewildering multiplicity of snow shovels has gone on display in practically every store in town. With winter coming, you can buy a snow shovel in a grocery store, a drugstore, a sporting goods store. Snow shovels are hawked with special fervor at those curious hybrid establishments known as home centers. (In more plainspoken times they were called hardware stores and lumberyards.) And what snow shovels they are! There are snow shovels that look like shovels, there are others that look like really large dental tools, there are even snow shovels that look like Eskimo perambulators. There are snow shovels with straight handles, snow shovels with bent handles; with fat blades, with thin blades; with D grips, with T grips. Some snow shovels are plastic and cost a couple of bucks; others are so expensive that it seems wrong to expose them to a substance, like snow, that comes for free. What to do?

It took me a number of winters to discover that very often the best snow shovel is not a shovel at all. Get yourself a simple broom, one with long, stiff straw. A broom will take care of better than half the snow you'll get in a winter, and it won't break your back, burst your heart, or dig up your grass by mistake. For cleaning snow off the car, the broom is far superior to the shovel because it can't scratch your paint job. And if you are equipped with a broom and you should, at last, get a fall of snow too deep for your broom to overcome, you can simply hop on it and fly south until you get to a latitude where snow is unknown and the home centers sell only those shovels that come with pails for use at the beach.

A FOOT of snow or maybe a little more fell last night, but then the sky cleared quickly, and now, midmorning, the sun lies over the perfect new snow as smooth and even as a beach. In a minute I'll start shoveling out.

The task of shoveling out at my house consists of making two main lines: the New York Central, a straight shot of about fifty feet from the house to the woodshed; and the Grand Trunk, an eighty-foot path to the compost and ash piles which jogs around a big old tree and a picnic table. There are also spur lines connecting those lines to other doors. The total distance is less than 150 feet. Shoveling out, done right, might take half an hour, given good snow.

Today the snow is good. It's not so dry that it fills in behind you like the sands of the trackless Sahara, and it's not so wet that you feel as though you were shoveling concrete. Rather, it's snow that cuts like a wedding cake, yielding sharp, clean blocks. In a few minutes the Central is finished, and I embark upon the Grand Trunk.

From the back door I sight upon the ash pile and begin to shovel. Slip the blade under the snow, lift, toss, step, slip the blade again. Presently I stop, straighten up, feel my pulse. It is probably no faster than the pulse of a hummingbird who is about to be presented at the Court of St. James's. I slow down a bit, but I keep at it. Up ahead, I see, the ash pile I'm aiming for has veered several points to starboard. I correct course passing the picnic table. How strangely difficult it is to make a true straight line over land, and what a feat of those old Roman engineers who laid paved roads straight as a rule across all Europe. They didn't have to shovel snow, though, did they? Did they? Well, I'll soon be done.

IT is often in February that I find myself shoveling snow away from the windows of my house to let some light into the interior gloom. Some years, though, window shoveling time comes in January, even December. That's how I know how tough a winter it's being. Some years window shoveling never comes at all. We had a winter like that about four years ago.

This house is a Cape Cod cottage. It has four windows in each of the two long walls under the slope of the roof. The windows are about chest-high, outside. The ground below the windows receives whatever snow falls on it directly, and it also receives the snow that slides off the roof. The area of the roof is by a good bit the largest exposed plane of the house — six hundred square feet, each side. That's a lot of snow. In a good year it doesn't take long for the snow to build up to the bottoms of the windows, then to the bottoms of the upper sashes. Most years, the snow reaches the eaves of the house, hiding the windows and making it dark inside. It's like living in an igloo. You can go crazy this way. So I shovel out the windows.

I pick a bright day. I climb the snow hill in front of the house until I'm at the level of the tops of the snowed-in windows. Standing about at the height of the eaves, I take a minute to look out at the view from up there; it's not an altitude I'm accustomed to, and I can see a lot, especially in winter, that I miss from nine feet below.

I begin to shovel. Soon the tops of the windows emerge. I go slowly, probing with my shovel for glass. (I've shoveled out the windows for some years with no mishap, but someday I know I'll drive the shovel right through one.) Soon the windows are clear. Inside, the inhabitants gather at the windows, blinking at the day like survivors of a mine disaster at the moment of their deliverance.

THE snowshoer in the winter woods is a locomotor contradiction: an elephant in flight. He flounders along strapped onto a pair of platforms whose design and construction have evolved perversely through centuries to make effective walking clumsy, labored, and difficult. If the outdoorsman owns the popular "bear paw" snowshoe, he is obliged to hold his legs as though he were on the back of a fat old horse and to walk like a ruptured gander. If he has chosen a longer, slimmer shoe with a tail, he will trip over his heels and kick himself in the bottom, and his turning radius will be comparable to that of the S.S. *France*. In either case the snowshoer will hang up on the brush, sideslip hopelessly if he descends a hill obliquely and fall on his face if he goes straight at it, plunging awkwardly on at the head of a trail that might have been made by an army tank.

But consider now the snowshoer's advantage: snowshoes make difficult what without them is impossible. In much of the hilly woodland around my house the snow can lie as deep as a man's chest. Skis aren't practical in the thick woods. Even a snowmobile can't get you where snowshoes — clumsily — can. They're the only game in town. And when you accept that, you see the best fun of snowshoeing: the flight. You are up on top of all that snow, walking through the air over the white surface like a spirit over the water. The little fir beside your trail, waist-high, is the top of a ten-foot tree. The branches of the maples you must duck are where the birds will nest in the spring. You have traded grace and ease of progress for access to a new world; and which of us who watched our brothers in the Apollo program twenty years ago would refuse that trade? The Apollo astronauts walked heavily, clumsily, like snowshoers. But they were walking on the moon.

Change

A WEEK of cold coming straight down from the Pole: −20 by night, zero at noon, everything freezes solid, and the air makes the inside of your head hurt. You can burn everything you've got that will burn — wood, oil, gas, books, feathers, the cats — and still you won't feel warm. It won't last forever, though, and when the cold drop at last relents, it is a remarkable thing how much satisfaction will flow from a very little warming. The fundamental optimism of animal life is nowhere better displayed.

When the temperature has been down below zero for a few days, it doesn't take much mercury to produce a change of weather in the heart. Let the thermometer hit 10 degrees on the high side, and the birds seem to stand up straighter, the squirrels to breathe more easily. As for the people, they practically fall down from relief, especially the young. They forget their coats, emerge in shirtsleeves. Anywhere over 15 degrees, and they'll go about in bathing suits.

The reaction apparently depends not on the high temperature attained but on the interval between the high and low temperatures. Friends of mine in St. Paul, where the winter regularly gets down colder than it does in New England, report that no Minnesota kid worth his or her citizenship wears a coat when the temperature is above −10; at zero you are hard-pressed to keep them decent. The same fact shows that the phenomenon is national and not a mere regionalism.

For some reason it doesn't work on the warm end of the year. In August, a week in the nineties doesn't make a day at 82 seem cold; it doesn't drive the young indoors to shiver around the stove. They take their relief when they need it.

TOWARD the end of February, as the season begins to commence to turn, every dooryard, every meadow, every wood is full of clocks. The winter buds are fat on the trees, and the brooks are running under the ice. Chickadees switch from the *dee-dee-dee* song that gives them their name to the peculiar, monotonous chant — two notes with the stress on the first — with which they encourage the spring. It sounds like "*come* on, *come* on, *come* on." On the farms the lambs are being born, and at night the shepherd's flashlight bobs along back and forth between the house and the barn. The shepherd hasn't had six hours sleep together all through the month.

The tops of south-facing hills keep the sunlight longer and longer now against the night, and dusk lingers nearly until six o'clock. Every meadow is a sundial, the shadows of the trees along its edge reaching farther as each afternoon brings a little more sun. If you cared to keep such minute watch in your own backyard, you could tell the day without the aid of a calendar by measuring the angle of a tree's shadow at a certain hour or seeing how the sunlight lies in the open doorway of a shed.

The best timepiece at my house is Zinnia, an old calico cat. She is slow these days. Fifteen years ago she was a kitten, but that was in a city miles to the south. Zinnia lives in a snug house in the lee of a building. She doesn't get out much. In the dark of winter, days may pass without her appearing at all. But on a bright afternoon in February, Zinnia will climb up on the snowbank near her house and go happily to sleep in the sun. She takes gratefully to the increasing light, and when the sun gets past the middle of the month, she's there to meet it. If Zinnia is asleep on the snow, it's nearly March.

"Science"

A BIG storm is blowing in from the north. The wind rises and bears down on this house, which is not much protected on the north. It's an old house, and as it takes the weight of the wind, its boards and timbers creak and crack as if it were one of the clipper ships that were making news when the house was — even then not new — but not yet old.

This house was built a little more than two hundred years ago by a race of frontier farmer-artisans, a people whose skill, strength, and sheer capacity for hard work I can imagine only imperfectly. Those who built the house knew exactly what they were about. They put up a simple rectangle forty feet by thirty, perched on an enormous rock pile in the cellar, the chimney foundation. It's a convenient house, it even has a kind of plain beauty, but two hundred years is a long time. There is not a right angle anywhere in the house. Each door is a parallelogram, and the tilting floors roll like a gentle sea. The entire structure, in fact, is no longer a box but rather a shallow pyramid, the apex held aloft by the massive chimney foundation at the center of the house while the corners settle inexorably into the ground. The ground has been pulling at this house for a long time, pulling on its footings, on its sills, on its roof, drawing it down further into its destined entropy. With jacks and braces, posts and paint, its owners, including me, have resisted time, and we will go on doing so. But the contest never ends. And so if I were to decorate the lintel of this house I would do so not with the date of its rearing, but with this equation: $S^2 - S^1 = q/T$. Engineers will recognize a statement of the Second Law of Thermodynamics, which, if I understand it, rightly, says that everything goes to hell unless you prop it up, and which is all the physics an owner of this house will ever need to know.

IN the spring of 1919, from Príncipe Island off the Guinea Coast of West Africa, where he had gone on a scientific expedition to observe a total eclipse of the sun occurring at the time, Sir Arthur Stanley Eddington, a British astronomer, announced that his observations indicated a tiny shift in the apparent positions of certain stars near the sun. The seeming displacement of the stars amounted to no more than a fraction of a degree, but it made a mighty noise in the scientific world. For Eddington's observations offered the first experimental proof of the General Theory of Relativity, which Albert Einstein had introduced in 1916. Einstein held that light has mass and is therefore subject to gravity. It followed that light rays passing a massive body like the sun ought to be bent by the gravitational attraction of that body. That bending of the light issuing from stars visible during the eclipse was what A. S. Eddington saw in Africa; the shift in the stars' apparent positions was due to their light's being deflected as it passed the sun. Einstein had predicted the shift to within 0.03 second of arc of what Eddington found. The General Theory of Relativity was a theory no longer.

If Eddington had only checked with me, I could have saved him a lot of travel. To be convinced of the truth of the theory of relativity, no one need go any farther than New England in January — the longest thirty-one days of the year. The other long months — May, August, October, and the rest — accomplish their thirty-one days in thirty-one days. In January the same span of time lasts far longer. Why, in 1961, January lasted until the afternoon of April 10. A lot depends on who's looking, just as Einstein said; and you don't need an African eclipse or a fancy sextant to prove that if you've waited out January in the North.

Tools & Tasks

SOMETIME after the first of the year, in a dry storm of needles, the Christmas tree is hauled out of the house and discarded — but how? In New York, I understand, they simply take their old trees out to the street and leave them at the curb, much as you'd bounce an obstreperous drunk out of a bar-room. The idea is that the Department of Sanitation will come around and take the trees away. It does, and the New York way with last year's Christmas trees works fine for everybody. Around here, however, the Department of Sanitation is me, and that puts a whole different spin on the ball, you see.

I don't have a big enough car to let me take our old tree to the town dump, which is where the Department of Sanitation takes the other trash in this neighborhood. I guess I could simply toss the tree over the bank across the road, but I won't. Getting rid of Christmas trees that way seems sloppy to me. We have tried other measures. We've burned our tree in a fiery reprise of its role at Christmastime. We've broken it up for kindling wood. One year we hung the old tree with bits of bread and crackers and hunks of beef suet and stuck it out in the yard for winter birds to visit. The birds didn't much like their new tree. I believe they knew it was a fake.

Now after New Year's I take the tree out of the house, through the yard, and up into a little meadow. There I slyly plant it, shoving its end deep into the snow. I put the tree well out in the meadow, away from the woods that surround the open. From the house the sight of the green little tree standing out there where no tree stood yesterday is momentarily startling, which is the effect I aimed at in putting it where it is: to break up the landscape a little; to change things, but not too much; to bring Birnam Wood to Dunsinane.

AFTER the January Thaw comes the February Freeze. Both are mythical events, really, or at least they are movable events. The January Thaw may take place in December or it may not take place at all, and the February Freeze can put a stop to the quickenings of March. A late freeze will come this month in most years, though, and if you're sick of winter this is the one that will break your heart.

The February Freeze comes as you realize that the year at last is turning toward spring. You notice that the sun isn't quite a winter sun anymore. It is warm these days, and it makes real shadows, which the sun of December never does. The sun gets into the trees, softening, limbering, awakening buds. At the ends of their gray branches the smallest twigs show mellower pinks, yellows, greens. The trees stretch their arms. The sun gets into the snow and begins to break it down. It gets into the frozen roads. They soften, and to a depth of an inch or so their surface turns to mud. The sun gets into you, too. It gets into your heart and tissues and into your mind. It prepares your soul for spring.

Comes the February Freeze. The trees close up like traps. They freeze inside; their branches creak again. The snow that was softening goes as hard and tight as a concrete sidewalk; you can jump up and down on it. The roads that were going to mud freeze solid again, and taking a car on them is like trying to drive a train over the wrong-sized tracks. It's hard, when you had thought winter was ending, to have it all back again.

Cheer up. You were right. The sun is warmer. The snow froze and the roads froze, but you didn't freeze. The sun is still preparing your soul for spring, and soon it will be back at the snowbanks and the ice. The meadows will turn gray, then brown, then green. Winter will be a memory. You were right to rejoice.

SPRING SNOW

INDEX

ABOUT THE AUTHOR

Castle Freeman, Jr., has written the "Farmer's Calendar" for *The Old Farmer's Almanac* since 1981. His articles have appeared in numerous magazines, including *Yankee, The Atlantic Monthly, Harrowsmith Country Life,* and *Country Journal.* He is the author of *The Brides of Ambrose and Other Stories.* He lives in Newfane, Vermont.